It's That Deep

The Spiritual Conflict between Divine Nine Membership,

Secret Societies, and Following Jesus

Shamari Pitts

Copyright © 2024 Shamari Pitts

All rights reserved.

ISBN-13: 979-8-9915505-0-5

Unless otherwise indicated, all Scripture quotations are taken from the New King James Version of the Bible.

Any copyrighted material contained herein is for: criticism, comments, news reporting, teaching, scholarship, and research, all used in accordance with the Fair Use Exception 17 USC 107.

All ritual references are direct quotes from the various sources that are cited in the Footnotes section. Superscripts can be found in each section denoting quoted ritual content. Some wordings were paraphrased by the providers of the sources (such as online PDFs) or may have slight variations due to each organization's Ritual Books being printed in multiple editions over many years. Citations for Footnote #20 were only sourced from the online/digital source that is referenced.

DEDICATION

This book is dedicated to the Body of Christ, His beloved bride. May we continue transforming into the image and likeness of our Savior, spotless and ready for His coming. God bless you ♡

CONTENTS

Acknowledgments   i

Foreword by Carlisa May   ii

Preface   v

Introduction   vii

I. Rituals *(Altars and Bowing)*   1

II. Deities *(Association with Greek, Egyptian, and Roman gods)*   22

III. Hymns and Chants   42

IV. Adding and Subtracting from the Word of God   53

V. Light *(Claims of 'The Light;' Only Jesus is the Light of the World)*   59

VI. Spiritual Binding   64

VII. Concluding Thoughts   75

    Things that Contradict Scripture   75

    Witchcraft, Pagan, and Occult Practices   87

    Secrets Only Belong to the Lord   90

VIII. Freemasonry *(History, Continued)*   95

IX. Common Questions, Statements, and Rebuttals   116

X. Resources and Steps to Denounce/Renounce   132

    Denouncing Testimonies by *Ashton Asres* and *Akira Ca'Pri*   138

    References   140

    Footnotes   148

    About the Author   152

ACKNOWLEDGMENTS

Publishing a first book is not a simple task. At least in this year of 2024, I did not necessarily plan to become an author! It may not have been in my plans, but it was certainly in God's. I am so grateful to God and for every person who has helped me release this work, to release what God had given me.

Thank you to every person who has supported me and this book. Thank you to everyone who has pushed, encouraged, and motivated me. Thank you, even, to friends, family, and peers who may have disagreed with the content but were open to discourse, sharing perspectives, and still supported me.

Thank you to my beautiful family: especially my parents, aunts, and uncles. Thank you to my church family as well, Faith Filled Church. I am surrounded by amazing men and women of God who are doing amazing things for the Kingdom and even publishing many books themselves.

I would like to express my gratitude and appreciation for: my pastors whose coaching, guidance, and encouragement means so much, *Pastor Joshua Okpara* and *Pastor Charmecia Okpara* of Faith Filled Church, Lewisville, TX; my powerful sister in Christ and new friend, *Carlisa May*, who boldly wrote the Foreword and provided much insight during this process; *Ashton Asres* for sharing his personal denouncing testimony with power and humility; *Akira Ca'Pri* for sharing her personal denouncing testimony with excellence and creativity; *Jada Spruill* of Saphar's Page, Editing & Writing, the wonderful woman of God who edited my manuscript; and my dear friend, *Henry Madubuike* of Visuals by Henry, for designing my book cover.

I could not have accomplished this alone; thank you, thank you, thank you! I pray that God receives glory from this project and that He is glorified in all your lives.

FOREWORD

BY CARLISA MAY

When God calls someone to speak on something that is contrary to what the world would deem as acceptable, the warfare tends to come. There are some people who would likely say that if you were "not a part of this," you do not have the ability to speak on that subject. Then, there are others who would say "it is not a big deal; mind your business." Lastly, there are those who simply will ignore the warnings and stay in a place of ignorance or lack of knowledge. I can truly say that Shamari is none of these types of people.

The interesting thing about God is that He will pick who He wants to be His mouthpiece. Regardless of age, gender, race, ethnicity, etc., God will choose His servants that unapologetically follow His lead. In this case, I believe the Lord chose right to have Shamari be the one to speak this truth in "It's That Deep." The truth is– Black Greek Letter Organizations (BGLOs) are not of God, no matter how many members say that they are. The truth is– you cannot serve two masters. The truth is– this topic might offend some people; some people might be bitter, but I want to encourage you that it is the truth that sets you free.

From my personal experience, as a former member of Delta Sigma Theta, I had to learn a hard truth. The truth was that I was serving both

God and the enemy unknowingly. This truth, when the Lord revealed to me the root and foundation of Delta, was hard for me to accept.

In 2022, I asked the Lord to reveal anything that I was connected to that was not of Him. That prayer was answered swiftly, but it took me about two years to truly be obedient and renounce my membership due to fear, ignorance, and simply just not wanting anything to do with Delta. I completely cut off my ties with the organization by not attending or participating in any events, but spiritually, I was still in covenant with the enemy by way of Minerva, the goddess attached to Delta.

I officially renounced my membership to Delta on February 27, 2024. It was not too long after, when I posted about renouncing on my Instagram story, that Shamari reached out to interview me for a book she was writing regarding the history and roots of the entire Divine 9 organizations. Unbeknownst to me at the time, the Lord gave Shamari every step to take in authoring this book from personal interviews, research, quoted material from hard copies of each ritual book, and more.

Here's the truth, you must be ready to receive **_all_** the information that is shared in this book. Many people have and will continue to question why "black people" or "black culture" is constantly being attacked, but my question would be: have we exalted blackness and black culture above Kingdom? If you read this book with the perspective that because Shamari was not in a BGLO, she has no right to speak on these things, I would encourage you to read Paul's letters. Paul addressed those who were in error even when he did not participate in the same things they did because he *loved* them and cared about their soul and eternity. Paul cared about how the Church reflected Jesus. As Christians and disciples, we should care about how we represent Christ also.

This is not a foreword or a book to shame or condemn you, but I will encourage you to pray before you read the rest of the pages of this book. On these pages, you will see in detail about each organization: the rituals and the god(s) associated that members serve, along with biblical wisdom and knowledge that makes the truth plain.

The Holy Spirit inspired this book, and the Holy Spirit is the One who will lead you to all truth. Shamari is the servant chosen by God to release the word of the Lord concerning the deception with these organizations. This is a book that will spark conversations many are afraid to have concerning being a disciple and a BGLO member: is it acceptable in God's eyes? This book provides the true perspective. This is a book that will break generational curses. This is a book that will lead to freedom.

I am praying that the truth will be revealed to you as you read through these pages.

PREFACE

My name is Shamari, and I am here to share some information— a compilation of scriptures and notes regarding the transgressive and spiritual conflict with Christianity and secret societies, specifically Black Greek Lettered Organizations (BGLOs).

> As you read this presentation, I pray you encounter the presence and voice of God as His truth is revealed. May your heart and eyes continue to be open and receptive to the heart and will of our Father. I pray, according to Colossians 1:9-10, **"that you may be filled with the knowledge of His will in all wisdom and spiritual understanding; that you may walk worthy of the Lord, fully pleasing Him, being fruitful in every good work and increasing in the knowledge of God."**

This document prominently addresses the National Pan-Hellenic Council (NPHC)/Divine 9 (D9) organizations. However, these notes also apply to Freemasonry, The Order of the Eastern Star, secret societies in non-Western cultures, and other (not necessarily all) fraternal organizations. I have not researched all of the Pan-Hellenic Council (PHC) or the multicultural organizations at this time, but if you are a follower of Jesus Christ and a part of either of those, I encourage you to still seek the Lord's will regarding your membership and any ceremonial rituals you may have performed.

As an HBCU alumna and relative to members of D9 organizations, I absolutely had an interest in joining Greek life. As excited as I was about the intake process, I questioned if it was of God. I was so curious about the secrecy that I started researching the hidden parts, such as various ritual books (pdf versions found online) and intake processes.

Spiritually, a question I had was, "Do these organizations have spiritual implications and roots?"

During my sophomore year after attending a Rush meeting, God gave me a dream showing me that my future children would be spiritually oppressed and afflicted if I decided to pursue membership, spiritually binding myself with the organization of interest. I didn't even know as much about the spiritual realm at that time. I began gradually compiling all of this information together as I learned more about **spiritual covenants:** legal agreements that one makes in the spiritual realm. Rituals, altars, kneeling, and chants—as performed in all the D9 organizations—are open gateways to forming demonic covenants, causing the Believer to unknowingly or knowingly commit idolatry, and/or be susceptible to attacks from the kingdom of darkness. Open doors lead to demonic access. Also, participation and membership hinder Christians from walking in the *fullness* of God.

The Divine 9 Greek Lettered Organizations ("GLO's," along with many other GLO's) are not of God, and it is completely against His will for Christians to be a part of them.

Yes, God gave me a dream; this was a personal encounter. But He also gave me scripture, the Word of God, which is applicable to us all. You will find those scriptures in the proceeding text(s).

I present biblical reasonings of why it is necessary to discuss this topic in the Body of Christ. Following are relevant terms and definitions that will be defined such as "Divine" Nine, Hellenism ('Pan-Hellenic'), Ritual, Altar, Hymn, Worship, Idolatry, Secret Society, and Freemasonry. There are then chapters expounding on Rituals (altars and bowing); deities associated with each of the organizations; hymns and chants (especially pledging "All of My Love" to something other than God); examples of how the rituals manipulate, twist, add and subtract from the Word of God; how many of the organizations claim to be The Light (which is blasphemous to Jesus Christ, the only Light); and how membership leads to being spiritually bound. Concluding this book is an overview of general examples of how being in the organizations is contradictory to a life of following Jesus, of subtle witchcraft, of paganism, and of occultic practices involved in initiation, along with how secrets and mysteries belong to the Lord. There is also an expounded section on Freemasonry, as most, especially D9, fraternal and sororal organizations have clear roots in Freemasonry. In addition, I address common questions, statements, and rebuttals such as oaths and rituals being involved in professional fields (and many things outside of Greek life) and many pastors and Christian leaders being Greek, to name a few. Lastly, you will find real-life testimonies, resources, and steps to renounce and denounce one's organization.

INTRODUCTION

SCRIPTURES AND THOUGHTS TO
CONSIDER FOR THE PURPOSE OF THIS BOOK:

God continues sanctifying the Believer (individually) and the Church (collectively).

> "For by one offering He has perfected forever those who are being sanctified." – Hebrews 10:14

> "that He might present her to Himself a glorious church, not having spot or wrinkle or any such thing, but that she should be holy and without blemish." – Ephesians 5:27

As members in the body of Christ, we are called to encourage one another to continue in good works and living righteously for God.

> "And let us consider one another in order to stir up love and good works, not forsaking the assembling of ourselves together, as is the manner of some, but exhorting one another, and so much the more as you see the Day approaching."
> – Hebrews 10:24-25

If you see a brother or sister in Christ that is in continual sin, you should correct them in gentleness and love. The Bible indeed tells us to judge, but to judge righteously and without hypocrisy.

> "My brothers and sisters, if one of you should wander from the truth and someone should bring that person back, remember this: Whoever turns a sinner from the error of their way will save them from death and cover over a multitude of sins."

– James 5:19-20

"What business is it of mine to judge those outside the church? Are you not to judge those inside?" – 1 Corinthians 5:12

"Brothers and sisters, if someone is caught in a sin, you who live by the Spirit should restore that person gently."
– Galatians 6:1a

"judge with righteous judgment." – John 7:24b

"And why do you look at the speck in your brother's eye, but do not consider the plank in your own eye? Hypocrite! First remove the plank from your own eye, and then you will see clearly to remove the speck from your brother's eye."
– Matthew 7:3, 5

The works of darkness must be exposed.

"And have no fellowship with the unfruitful works of darkness, but rather expose them." – Ephesians 5:11

When God gives a watchman a warning, it is to be spoken to His people— for the sake of the people and the watchman.

> "Nevertheless if you warn the righteous man that the righteous should not sin, and he does not sin, he shall surely live because he took warning; also you will have delivered your soul."
> – Ezekiel 3:21

***

Relevant Terms and Definitions

The following are terms directly associated with the NPHC and are in contradiction with scripture and God's commandments. It will serve as context for the following information provided in the document.

1. **"Divine"** Nine
   - Religion
     - of, relating to, or proceeding directly from God or a god
     - being a deity
       - *The divine Savior*
     - directed to a deity
       - *Divine worship*[1]

   - HEAVENLY, GODLIKE[1]

So, we must ask, what deity or heavenly being does the name refer to? *The 'Divine' in Divine Nine is not referring to Yahweh, the only God we should be acknowledging. And we are only meant to worship Him in spirit and truth, not in mixture.*

2. **Hellenism** (e.g. "Pan-Hellenic")
   - ➤ <u>devotion</u> to or <u>imitation</u> of <u>ancient Greek</u> thought, customs, or styles[2]
   - ➤ Greek <u>culture</u>; the national character or nature of the Greeks, esp. the ancient Greeks[3]

Hellenism also refers to the culture of modern and ancient Greece. This is where many of the rites/rituals and practices come from. We should not be devoting ourselves to or imitating the ways of the world and the ancient, secular cultures in which God's people, like the Israelites, were commanded not to follow. **"Do not learn the way of the Gentiles (or 'heathens') ... for the customs of the peoples are futile…"** – *Jeremiah 10:2-3* | **"When you enter the land the LORD your God is giving you, do not learn to imitate the detestable ways of the nations there."** – *Deuteronomy 18:9* | **"the things which the Gentiles sacrifice they sacrifice to demons and not to God, and I do not want you to have fellowship with demons."** – *1 Corinthians 10:20*

3. **Ritual**
   - ➤ a religious or solemn ceremony consisting of a series of actions performed according to a prescribed order[4]

All of the D9 organizations include rituals in their initiation ceremonies. Most of the initiation ceremonies include lit candles, kneeling on something (such as a pillow), and an altar.

4. **Altar**
    - a block, <u>table</u>, stand, or other raised structure with a flat top used as the focus for a religious ritual, especially for making sacrifices or offerings to <u>a god or gods</u>[5]

5. **Hymn**
    - a <u>religious</u> song or composition that <u>praises God or a god</u>[6]
    - a <u>religious</u> song or poem of <u>praise to God or a god</u>[6]

    Biblical Greek Definition
    - a song in the praise of gods, heroes, conquerors[7]

A hymn should only be sung to our God, Yahweh. All 9 NPHC organizations have at least one hymn sung TO the name of the organization, often addressing it [the organization] as "Thy;" "Thou;" "Thee;" etc. The demonic agenda is to get the believer to give their praise to false gods, or simply a thing that is not God.

"Let the word of Christ dwell in you richly in all wisdom, teaching and admonishing one another in psalms and <u>hymns</u> and spiritual songs, singing with grace in your hearts to the Lord." – *Colossians 3:16 NKJV*

Be careful of what you sing, and who you are singing to.

6. **Worship**
    - ➢ a form of religious practice with its creed and ritual[8]
    - ➢ revere (a deity), conduct religious rites[8]
        rite = synonym for *ritual*
    - ➢ To perform, or take part in, an act of worship directed towards (a god, etc.); to venerate with appropriate <u>acts, rites, or ceremonies</u>[9]

Satan's crafty deception has caused believers to worship other 'gods' unknowingly. This is not a matter of people individually "putting their organization before God" (although that is sometimes a real issue) or the idolatry of 'caring' about their organization more than God. This is a discussion of participation in practices, worship, and idolatry that is ancient and deeply rooted, again, often done unknowingly or unintentionally. As noted in the definition, taking part in an act of worship is indeed worship.

7. **Idolatry**
    - ➢ extreme admiration, love, or reverence for something or someone[10]

        biblically, for something other than God

8. **Secret Society**

    "any of a large range of membership organizations or associations that utilize secret initiations or other rituals and whose members often employ unique oaths, grips (handshakes), or other signs of recognition. Elements of secrecy may vary from a mere password to elaborate rituals, private languages, costumes, and symbols. The term may be applied to such widely divergent groups as U.S. college fraternities and sororities, the Ku Klux Klan, and international Freemasonry as well as to similar phenomena in ancient or pre-colonial cultures.

Among the earliest secret societies of which historical evidence exists were the mystery religions of ancient Egypt, Greece, and Rome, which had secret rites, initiations, and revelations of still more ancient wisdom. Among these were the cult of Dionysus, the keepers of the Eleusinian and Orphic mysteries, and the Pythagorean brotherhood."[11]

9. **Freemasonry**

the systems and institutions of the Freemasons. It is a fraternal organization, known as one of the world's oldest. It subtly promotes syncretism (fusion of multiple religious beliefs) as members must profess belief in a 'supreme being,' but from any faith background. The organization gives regard to the "Grand Architect of the Universe." Apparently, when the Freemasons meet in their lodges for prayer, the members pray to their own gods. It is often called a secret society and includes rituals and oaths. Many Greek-lettered fraternities and sororities in the United States have roots and ties to Freemasonry.[12]

Note. From Eric Cable at English Wikipedia, Public domain, via Wikimedia Commons

I. RITUALS: ALTARS AND BOWING

During initiation rituals, the organizations have the setup of an altar (whether explicitly called one or not) and an instruction to bow or kneel. There are also oaths, vows, hymns, and sometimes the speaking of scriptures in which the organization's name is substituted for/replacing God's name. There are spiritual laws we must understand. Any time an altar is erected, contact with a spirit or spirits is welcomed. Don't let the enemy deceive you. These ritualistic occurrences are one of the main proponents of Christians committing idolatry and spiritually binding themselves to demonic and occult-related spirits. "An altar is a means of an earthly being fellowshipping with a spiritual being," Pastor A.W. "Al" Barlow. An altar is a meeting point of two worlds, the divine (supernatural) and the natural. An altar is also either evil or godly/supported by Jesus. There is no in-between. Any time you see an altar, you must ask which category it belongs to.

Following this section on Rituals will be an in-depth example (by way of the Kappa Alpha Psi ritual) of an altar. This example is the most explicit one. Other organizations may name it a 'table' instead. The ceremonial lighting of candles usually takes place at these altars.

Kneeling/Bowing (and even pronouncing Oaths) during Rituals:

Exodus 20:5 – **"you shall not bow down to [them] nor serve them. For I, the Lord your God, am a jealous God…"**

Zephaniah 1:4-5 – "…I will cut off **every trace of Baal** from this place, the names of the idolatrous priests with the pagan priests– those who worship the host of heaven on the housetops; those who worship and **swear oaths by the Lord, but who ALSO swear by Milcom**"

2 Kings 17:7, 8; 29; 33-35 – "However every nation continued to make **gods of its own**, and put them in the **shrines** on the high places… and they had feared other gods, and had **walked in the statutes of the nations** whom the Lord had cast out from before the children of Israel… **They feared the Lord, yet** served their own gods–**according to the rituals of the nations from among** whom they were carried away. **To this day they continue practicing the former rituals**; they do not fear the Lord, nor do they follow their statutes or their ordinances, or the law and commandment which the Lord had commanded the children of Jacob, whom He named Israel, with whom the Lord had made a covenant and charged them, saying: 'You shall not fear other gods, **nor bow down** to them nor serve them nor sacrifice to them"

This particular passage from 2 Kings 17 blows my mind! It truly applies to our time today. These people indeed feared God, but they had mixture (as in the Zephaniah passage as well – swearing oaths by the Lord AND swearing oaths by [the god] Milcom). They followed the traditions, patterns, ordinances, and rituals of the various nations. Similarly to today, Believers are following ordinances that come from pagan Greek, Roman, and Egyptian cultures when the Lord has called us to be set apart.

Kneeling has always been a sign of reverence and submission.

> Kneel- *be in or assume a position in which the body is supported by a knee or the knees, as when praying or showing submission.*[13]

> In Asian cultures, for example, to bow is to humble oneself under someone/something. This is not as significant or recognized in western culture (making it easier to be deceived).

Bowing has always been a form of worship

> The Hebrew word translated for 'worship' is 'shachah,' meaning to bow down; to prostrate oneself; to depress

Food during Rituals:

In biblical times, covenants were often sealed by eating in fellowship. This is the same today in witchcraft, paganism, and Eastern religions (such as Hinduism) in which people offer food to their 'gods.' Rituals and pledging practices in which initiates must partake in food or drink have often caused Christians to participate in witchcraft. Food is a part of idolatry and covenant.

Even the Scriptures explain that partaking of food and drink at a pagan altar is to have fellowship and communion with the spirits (demons) behind those altars. Paul addressed Christian individuals in the Corinthian church who had fellowship with both the Lord and idols at the same time. The passage of scripture also suggests that there is a sole source of partaking: one bread, one cup (the Lord's). There is a ritual example listed where candidates are "partaking" of the symbolic "blood of the Fraternity."

1 Corinthians 10:14-22
"Therefore, my beloved, flee from idolatry. I speak as to wise men; judge for yourselves what I say. The cup of blessing which we bless, is it not the communion of the blood of Christ? The bread which we break, is it not the communion of the body of Christ? For we, though many, are one bread and one body; for we all partake of that one bread. Observe Israel after the flesh: **ARE NOT THOSE WHO EAT OF THE SACRIFICES PARTAKERS OF THE ALTAR?** What am I saying then? That an idol is anything, or what is offered to idols is anything? Rather, that the things which the **GENTILES** *(i.e. ancient Greek culture)* **SACRIFICE THEY SACRIFICE TO DEMONS and NOT TO GOD**, and I do not want you to have **FELLOWSHIP WITH DEMONS**. <u>You cannot drink the cup of the Lord and the cup of demons; you cannot partake of the Lord's table and of the table of demons.</u> Or do we **PROVOKE THE LORD TO JEALOUSY?** Are we stronger than He?"

Deuteronomy 32:38-39
"Who ate the fat of their sacrifices, and drank the wine of their drink offering? Let them rise and help you, and be your refuge.

'Now see that I, even I, am He. And there is no God besides Me.'"

Elements that "Activate" an Altar: Invoking Spirits and Covenants:

This is seen in occultic practices, African spirituality, Eastern spirituality, and secret societal rituals.

Elements you will see are a table/altar, candles (fire), and pictures of founders (usually deceased). Be mindful that many organizations honor their deceased founders by placing their pictures on the ceremonial altar. As you kneel down and take an oath, YOU are the sacrifice. I expound on this in the section: Witchcraft, Pagan and Occult Practices.

Mock examples based on descriptions and instructions found in multiple D9 ritual books:

Note. Image generated using Microsoft Copilot (Microsoft Copilot, 2024).

Note. Image generated using Microsoft Copilot (Microsoft Copilot, 2024).

Ritual Books: ***Kneeling*** and ***Bowing*** *during Initiation*

ALPHA PHI ALPHA

Section 11. -

The candidate shall **kneel** and **eat** the food prepared **by the gods** for ALPHA PHI ALPHA men. (Oysters or cold raw macaroni.)[14]

Section 12.

The candidate shall **drink** to the health of ALPHA PHI ALPHA. (Any drink not injurious, first agreeable and then disgusting to the taste. Two drinks.)[14]

ALPHA KAPPA ALPHA

Section: I. **Devotion** and Promise

To Our **Founders**, we **bow** (***candidates bow*** *their heads*).[15]

Section: II. Obedience

Basileus to Candidate: Are you willing to be **submissive** and in every way to **subjugate yourself to the highest authority**?
Pilot to Candidates. Repeat after me. "I Am." *Candidates:* I am.
Basileus: What proof have you.

Pilot to Candidates: Repeat after me: **"I show my submission by kneeling." Candidates kneel** *a few minutes. Nothing but silence prevails.*[15]

DELTA SIGMA THETA

*Page 237 of the 12th edition of the ritual book

There is an example of the setup of an altar (called a Ceremonial Table) in the Delta Sigma Theta initiation ceremony. Labeled by the numbers are:[16]

1. White <u>Candle</u> – Fundamental Principles
2. Red Candle –Torch of Wisdom
3. Sigma - Nine White Candles
4. Gavel
5. Candle Lighter
6. Candle Snuffer
7. Sorority Pins for Candidates
8. Prompter with Pledge in Large Print
9. Pen
10. <u>Pledge Signature Page</u>
11. Sorority Pin on Small White Cushion
12. White Candles for Candidates
13. Large Red <u>Pillow for Kneeling</u>
14. White Tablecloth
15. Delta Pennant

The Initiation Ceremony (pg. 194)

(*The President reads the pledge to the Candidates for consideration before it is recited individually. Each Candidate comes forward, one at a time* **to the Ceremonial Table**, **kneels**, *clasps both hands around the Torch of Wisdom and* **reads the pledge**...")

Candidate: I _____ (name), do promise in **the presence of the Eternal Spirit of Truth**....

(*While* **kneeling***, each Candidate signs the Pledge*...)[16]

As seen in this instruction, where there is an altar, there is a "presence."

PREPARATION FOR THE INITIATION CEREMONY (pg. 183, 12th edition)

- Ceremonial Table
- *Ritual*
- Large red cushion for kneeling[16]

ZETA PHI BETA

The Order of Ceremony

Basileus: Now you come to the <u>most serious part of the intake process</u>, **'taking the Oath'**. I admonish you to think of the words you will repeat after me. Think of what you are saying and what they mean, for truly, **this oath must be your constant guide for as long as you live,** 'Once a Zeta, always a Zeta.' Candidates, **kneel**, *place right hand on heart and left hand on the Bible. Repeat after me*...[17]

SIGMA GAMMA RHO

(Ritual)

Each candidate shall:

*a) **Kneel** before the Presiding Officer. b) Place both hands on the Bible*
*e) **Repeat the Pledge** led by the officer.*

The Presiding Officer shall light her candle.

Each pledge shall light her candle from the one held by the Presiding Officer. New Sorors, repeat in unison: I pledge myself to this Sorority to be true to its code, obey its rulings and keep faith with my sisters.[18]

OMEGA PSI PHI

Now inasmuch as you have complied with all the necessary requisites up to this point, and inasmuch as you have concurred with the ideals upon which this organization was founded and have evidenced no spirit other than the highest manhood, I shall ask you to **kneel** upon both your knees, place your left hand upon the Holy Bible which I here give you, raise your right hand toward the heavens and **repeat the oath** after me.

I, ... *full name,* uninfluenced by mercenary motives and imbued with a desire to serve mankind, in the name and presence of Almighty God, and of all I hold sacred, and under the sacred seal of the Omega Psi Phi Fraternity, do solemnly and sincerely promise and **swear absolute allegiance** to the Omega Psi Phi

Fraternity to uphold its name, preserve its honor, and guard zealously all that tends to promote its welfare. I further promise and swear that I shall always help a worthy distressed brother protect and help his family, warn him and them of any approaching danger, and hold his secrets when communicated to me as such, as sacred and inviolable in my breast as they were in his before communicated.

I further promise and swear that I will support the Constitution of the Omega Psi Phi Fraternity, maintain its standards, and never prove traitor to any trust imposed in me by the Omega Psi Fraternity; **binding myself** under no less a penalty if I forsake **thee, O Omega,** than to have my right hand lose her cunning and my tongue cleave to the roof of my mouth. So help me God, and keep me faithful and steadfast to the end of life's journey.[19]

IOTA PHI THETA

The Ceremony (The Centaur Ceremony)
D) THE INTAKE GROUP IS THEN **MADE TO KNEEL** IN A CIRCULAR POSITION...[29]

Going On Ceremony
Polaris: ...no great undertaking has been done without the aid of prayer. Young men, **kneel and pray together** that **your God(s) will watch over you and guide you along the way**.[29]

PHI BETA SIGMA

Arrangement of the Court (Physical Necessities)

The chief justice and the associate justices shall be seated around the **altar (table)**. The justices shall wear caps and gowns. The scribe and chaplain shall be seated at a table to the right or left of the altar. The sergeant-at-arms shall guard the door. The members shall be seated in such a way as to leave a passage-way from the door to the **altar**.
The lights shall be turned low, three lighted white candles being placed on the altar.[20]

Inferno - Wandering in Death Valley

The candidates are carried into a room in which is a table with human bones on it. Chairs, tin cans, etc., should be scattered about the floor in the path of the candidates. The candidates are led around the room a few times, making noises in the meantime. **Kneel the candidates before the table.** *A skull should be on the table so placed that the candidates can see it when the blindfolds are lifted a few seconds. The room should be lighted with a dim red light. Be sure that the candidates see no one when the blindfolds are lifted.*

Deputy, drinking the blood: Seekers, do you drink water? Pause for an answer. Tea? Coffee? Wine? or anything strong as a beverage? **In this cup is the blood of the Fraternity. Unless you partake of their blood, you are not fit to know them. Drink, you seekers.**
Gives the vessels of salt water to the candidates.

Deputy: Seekers, are you willing to give your time, energy, thought, and service to PHI BETA SIGMA for the uplift of mankind?
Candidates are told to answer.

Deputy: Then, **you must eat** worms of the earth as a test of service.

Give spaghetti.[20]

Inferno - Observing the Wonders of the Mountain

The Chief Justice rises and administers **the oath** *of membership to the candidates. The* **candidates <u>kneel</u> around the <u>altar</u>** *and place their hands on the Holy Bible and* **repeat the oath** *with the Chief Justice…*

Let the candidates remain in the same kneeling position.[20]

KAPPA ALPHA PSI

Reference of an altar is expounded upon in this section for Kappa Alpha Psi

Ritual *(for new initiates)*

PLEDGE CEREMONY

'Polemarch' instructs to **kneel** at the **Sacred Altar of Kappa Alpha Psi** and **repeat this oath**

> I, _____ in the presence of Almighty God and the members of Kappa Alpha Psi here assembled, and **at the Sacred Delphic Shrine**, do hereby **solemnly swear** that I shall keep secret forever all things that may transpire or be revealed to me during my initiation[21, 22]

PROCEDURE OF FORMAL MEETINGS

The **Altar** of Kappa Alpha Psi, which is the **Sacred Delphic Shrine**, shall be placed in the center of the room and covered with a crimson and cream coverlet.
The Holy Bible, opened to the Third Chapter of Proverbs shall be placed on the Altar.[21, 22]

Ending Pages -

The Vice Polemarch moves that the candidate is allowed to take the oath of allegiance and is duly received as a member. This motion is unanimously accepted. The candidate is **led to the altar, made to kneel** *and place his hand on the Bible and made to repeat the oath of allegiance:* I, _____, in the presence of Almighty God and the members of Kappa Alpha Psi here assembled, and at the **Sacred Delphic Shrine**, do hereby solemnly declare my unswerving allegiance to the Grand Fraternity of Kappa Alpha Psi, and do solemnly swear (or affirm) that I will ever respect, obey, and defend its Constitution and all of the regulations, emblems, and ritualistic work thereunto appertaining.[21, 22]

Kappa Constitution[22]

The Constitution and Statutes of Kappa Alpha Psi Fraternity, Inc. As amended at the 78th Grand Chapter Meeting - 2007

STATUTE 21. ELECTION OF CHAPTER OFFICERS

Section 6. All officers of each chapter and alumni association, prior to assuming their respective duties, shall **kneel at the Sacred Altar of Kappa Alpha Psi** and shall **repeat the following oath** which shall be administered by the presiding officer or a past Polemarch.

> ➢ I (each shall state his name) in the presence of Almighty God and the brothers of Kappa Alpha Psi here assembled, and **at the Sacred Delphic Shrine**, do solemnly affirm that I will faithfully execute the office of (each inductee shall state his office) and will to the best of my ability preserve, protect and defend the Ritual, Constitution, Statutes and all other regulations of Kappa Alpha Psi.[22]

STATUTE 37. INDUCTION OF NATIONAL OFFICERS

Section 2. All officers for induction into office shall **kneel at the sacred altar of Kappa Alpha Psi** and shall **repeat the following oath** with proper interpolations"

I (each inductee shall state his name) in the presence of Almighty God and the brothers of Kappa Alpha Psi here assembled, and **at the Sacred Delphic Shrine**, do solemnly affirm that I will faithfully execute the office of (each inductee shall state his office) and will to the best of my ability preserve, protect and defend the Ritual, Constitution, Statutes and all other regulations of Kappa Alpha Psi.[22]

***

Conflict of an Altar (Continued): Altar, Shrine, and Oracle

The purpose of an altar, according to a www.britannica.com (2011) article:

> "Raised structure or place used for sacrifice, worship, or prayer. Altars probably originated with the belief that objects or places (e.g., a tree or spring) were inhabited by spirits or deities worthy of prayers or gifts."

As stated previously, the definition of an altar is:

> a block, table, stand, or other raised structure with a flat top used as the focus for a religious ritual, especially for making sacrifices or offerings to a god or gods[5]

It is important to note that altars are used in the covenants of marriage: be it for the Church (His bride) that meets in the house of God or for two individuals coming together for marriage. At the altar, this is where you say, "I do." At the altar, you devote yourself to something. Earthly marriage is a sacrifice. Saying 'yes' to God is a sacrifice. When these organizations raise an altar to itself, you spiritually (and physically) offer yourself as a sacrifice. Some organizations' rituals use the words "I do." Most of the examples listed above say 'I do,' just in different words: in a pledge, in an oath, in a promise, in a swearing, or by saying, "I will," "I am," or "I submit."

I used the altar from Kappa's ritual as an example because it was one of the most explicit, and it raised further issues.

What is the Delphic Shrine (as the altar of Kappa Alpha Psi is called the Sacred Delphic Shrine), and what makes it 'sacred'?

Delphi is an ancient city in Greece. It is known for having the Temple of Apollo and the Oracle of Delphi (also named Pythia the high priestess). According to Britannica (2011), this was the "most famous ancient oracle, believed to deliver prophecies from the Greek god, Apollo."

Further down, that same article states, "The Pythia's counsel was most in demand to forecast the outcome of projected wars or political actions." As followers of Christ, we know that God shares His glory with no one and no thing. There is no thing or 'god' likened unto Him.

Isaiah 46:5 & 9-10 –

"To whom will you liken Me, and make Me equal
And compare Me, that we should be alike?
Remember the former things of old,

For I am God, and there is no other;

I am God, and there is none like Me,

Declaring the end from the beginning,

And from ancient times things that are not yet done,

Saying, 'My counsel shall stand,

And I will do all My pleasure.'"

Definition of an **"oracle"** according to the Merriam-Webster dictionary (n.d.):

- a person (as a priestess of **ancient Greece**) through whom **a god** is believed to speak.

    - a **shrine** in which **a deity** reveals **hidden knowledge** or the divine purpose through such a person[23]

        Deuteronomy 29:29, *"The secret things belong to the Lord our God, but the things that are revealed belong to us and to our children forever, that we may do all the words of this law."*

- the place where **a god speaks** through an oracle.

    - a person giving **wise** or authoritative decisions or

opinions[23]

But Job 12:13 says, **"To God belong wisdom and power; counsel and understanding are His."**

(Ritual)
The Strategus keeps the pledge walking until the members have arranged the assembly room to represent the Temple of Delphi. The room is arranged with an altar on which are a crucible of fire and a single candle. No one is in sight. The Oracle should be concealed in a nearby room or behind a curtain. The Strategus removes the blindfold at the door of the room and they approach the altar. As soon as they reach the altar, the Oracle asks the candidate what knowledge he is seeking.
The Strategus explains what is being sought.
The Oracle *rhymes:* Let him turn to the Sacred Altar, fire enflame, barley white cake offer in my name;
And then remaining at the Altar pray
That knowledge and high virtue may have sway
Over him and all his fellows evermore.
Till all are wafted to the Golden Shore.[21]

Strategus asks candidate whether he hears what is being said and upon a positive reply he is made to show his obedience. Strategus shows the glowing flame to candidate, gives him a dry cracker and directs him to crush and sprinkle this over coals.

The candidate is prompted to say the following: Great Oracle, confer I "hecatomb"
In this fair fane, the mighty Delphic Shrine,
White barley cake, not filthy goats and kine,
At thy great Altar on this Grecian stone.
That I may strive and successfully achieve
Some human good that greatly should be wrought;

That I may attain the manliness I ought
And merit here the noble Laurel Wreath,
Vouchsafe to me the knowledge that is meet
To fathom mysteries in this precious scroll,
These living truths and principles unfold
As thou has ever done to valiant Greeks.[21]

God is the One who knows all things. He is the One who counsels and declares what will be. Any oracle, diviner (of 'knowledge'), 'god,' or prophecy outside of the LORD and His Holy Spirit is idolatrous. And if it does not come from God/His kingdom, it comes from the kingdom of darkness. Therefore, these altars and shrines are only invoking demonic spirits. The Delphic Shrine, for example, was/is clearly used for worship in Greek culture. Even if a D9 initiate is not placing their personal belief or care towards these things, the spiritual realm is still being engaged, placing the initiate in covenant with darkness. Moreover, idolatry and worship are not solely about one's feelings or what one 'feels' in their heart for a thing, but what actions they partake in. The spiritual realm does not care about or regard so much a person's feelings. The enemy is simply looking for legal access or an open door.

II. DEITIES

ASSOCIATION WITH GREEK, EGYPTIAN, AND ROMAN GODS

God detests idolatry and association with false gods. Each D9 organization has association, honor, and/or significance tied to a deity or god.

Biblical Greek definition of *'idol'*:

- ➢ an image, likeness
    - i.e. whatever represents the form of an object, either real or imaginary
- ➢ the image of [a] heathen god
- ➢ a false god[24]

Exodus 20:4 – **"You shall not make for yourself a carved image—any likeness of anything that is in heaven above, or that is in the earth beneath, or that is in the water under the earth."**

Key words: *likeness of anything that is in heaven*

These Greek, Roman, and Egyptian deities are likened to heavenly creatures in the mythologies of those cultures and religions.

Also, a carved image, or a 'graven' image is a representation of a god that is used as an object for worship.

Exodus 23:13 – **"And in all that I have said to you, be circumspect and make no mention of the name of other gods, nor let it be heard from your mouth."**

***

List of gods/deities for each D9 org (following):

For most of these organizations, various gods and deities are displayed in different areas, such as the organizations' crests or coat of arms, paraphernalia, chants, hymns and rituals. But without even looking first at the rituals, **members are simply wearing the images of false gods**. The organizations often claim association with these gods. Don't be ignorant of Greek mythology. There are real principalities behind these idols that were and are worshiped in Greece, Rome, Babylon, etc. For instance, people do rituals and magic for Minerva today. A member may say that someone on the outside of the organization is unaware of the actual meaning, symbolism, or reason for use of the deities. Furthermore, it is said that they are only used symbolically, usually to symbolize a certain trait or virtue that the organization holds. It's understandable. For example, a balance scale represents justice. Yet, using false gods for representation is still wrong. No matter the symbolism, reason, or meaning, how can it be okay to wear the symbol of a god or deity on yourself at all (keeping in mind that the crests are worn over the heart)? For example, as a follower of Jesus, you would not willingly wear an image of Buddha on you, even if it's simply to use the image as a representation of wisdom, in which Buddha does represent. You would not make it an emblem and say, "Well, this just represents 'x,' not the actual religion of Buddhism." So, why do the gods associated with the Divine 9 organizations have an exception? It is no different.

Some ritual books even have the meaning of the symbols recorded. My mention of the deities below is not to misinterpret the meanings and what is documented in the rituals. No matter what the application and understanding of the symbols is, and how innocent it may seem, God is not pleased with His children (knowingly or unknowingly) honoring a deity. The Word says: **"Little children, keep yourselves from idols. Amen."** – 1 John 5:21

ALPHA PHI ALPHA: the Great Sphinx of Giza in Egypt

Note. From Louvre Museum, CC BY-SA 2.0
<https://creativecommons.org/licenses/by-sa/2.0>, via Wikimedia Commons

According to the Canadian Museum of History (n.d.), it represents Ra-Horakhty, an ancient Egyptian sun god.

Here is what Alpha Phi Alpha says about the Sphinx in their ritual book (pg. 1, year 1976 reprint):

> "The SPHINX of Gaza [spelled here with an 'a'] in Egypt, particularly its head, is **our emblem**…"
> "The SPHINX has stood silently and expectantly facing the East and the sunrise for thousands of years; it is thus a sentinel of the ages and a **keeper of their cherished secrets** (again, **Deuteronomy 29:29 says: 'The secret things belong to the Lord our God..')** thereby symbolizing **the mysteries** of the ALPHA PHI ALPHA FRATERNITY"[14]

> What the bible says about the East: It is related to the superstitions, sorceries, and divination of Babylon and Mesopotamia. **"For You have forsaken Your people, the house of Jacob, because they are filled with eastern ways." "Their land is also full of idols."** – Isaiah 2:6, 8. The Sphinx faces the east for the worship of the sun and sun gods.

> "…facing the rising sun. It was the focus of solar worship in the Old Kingdom" (Winston 2003).

The ritual book also lists the reasons they have chosen the Sphinx as the emblem. For example, the lion shape of the Sphinx simply represents strength. I, again, am not mentioning the Sphinx to misinterpret what is listed in the ritual book, but it is blasphemous for the reasons written at the start of this section.

ALPHA KAPPA ALPHA: Atlas, the Titan

In Greek mythology, titans are gods. They were just known as elders/pre-Olympian (as seen on the AKA Coat of Arms). Atlas, holding up the world, was the god of endurance and strength. "The Bearer of the Sky and Heavens," he held up the sky and heavens, and led war against Zeus according to mythology. The Greek word **atlaô** means **endurance**. In the *Alpha Kappa Alpha Initiation Ritual Handbook 1977 pg. 37*, it reads, **"The atlas signifies endurance and strength,"** under the "OUR COAT OF ARMS" section.[15] Satan is deceptive because the ritual book won't directly tell you that this represents the [false] god. If you look at the official Alpha Kappa Alpha Coat of Arms, Atlas is the symbol in the bottom right corner.

Psalms 104:5 - **"He set the earth on its foundations, so that it should never be moved."**

Proverbs 30:4- **"Who has ascended to heaven and come down? Who has gathered the wind in His fists? Who has wrapped up the waters in a garment? Who has established all the ends of the earth? What is His name, and what is His son's name? Surely you know!"**

Isaiah 66:1- **"Thus saith the LORD, The heaven is My throne, and the earth is My footstool."**

DELTA SIGMA THETA: Minerva, the Roman goddess of Wisdom

In Roman religion and mythology, Minerva is known as the goddess of wisdom and many other attributes.

Pallas Athena is the Greek version of this goddess.

For Delta Sigma Theta, she is the patron of the organization. She is seen at the center top of the Coat of Arms.

This is a false god/deity.

Quotes from the organization about Minerva:

"That is why Minerva, the goddess of wisdom, is our sorority mentor."

— DELTA SIGMA THETA SORORITY, INC., GRAND CHAPTER, MEMBERSHIP INTAKE PROGRAM, 1987-1990, p.106

"Our founders were well aware of the need to transfuse the ideals of Greek moral virtues with the later concepts of brotherhood and love"

— DST Grand Chapter Candidate Syllabus, 1987-1990, pg.30

"Minerva, the goddess of wisdom, one of the strongest and most admirable goddesses of antiquity, was chosen by the Founders as the patron of the Sorority. She serves merely as a SYMBOLIC representation of desirable archetypical attributes of mind, body, and SPIRIT. The goddess' name derives from the ancient roots for "mind" and her domain was intellectual.

Minerva was also said to be the inventor of music. It is fitting, therefore, that the exemplary attributes associated with Minerva be influential in the minds and spirits of the Sorors holding the responsibility of planning and conducting all intake activities, including induction, and orientation of new members into Delta Sigma Theta. These Sorors comprise the Minerva Circle" (Hatchett, 2005).

Part II - Symbols - Handbook pg. 207

The Sorority Crest:

"The Delta Sigma Theta Sorority Crest is Delta Sigma Theta Sorority's official Coat of Arms. The crest is a composite idea expressing graphically the Sorority's Public Motto: "Intelligence is the Torch of Wisdom." **Minerva (Pallas Athena) the Goddess of Wisdom,** is atop the shield which bears the torch, the sword, the staff and the three Greek letters. The sword, representing **truth**, is a part of Minerva's symbolism."[16]

The Sorority Emblem:

"The Sorority emblem is the Goddess Minerva (Pallas Athena), Goddess of Wisdom."[16]

More on 'wisdom'—

The Initiation Ceremony (combination of 1969 Ritual and 12th edition):

"*Vice President:* Our [Public] Motto is: "Intelligence is the Torch of Wisdom." Behold the Torch of Wisdom. *Indicates Torch/She points to the red candle.* It burns whenever Delta women are assembled, and **guides our footsteps** as we work **in the name of our Sorority**. As college educated women, holding the torch aloft, we seek to use our trained intellect toward the advancement of intellectual, social and spiritual pursuits in the service of mankind."[16, 25]

Job 12:13 – "But [only] with Him are [perfect] wisdom and might; He [alone] has [true] counsel and understanding." (AMP)

Proverbs 2:6 – **"For the LORD gives wisdom: out of his mouth comes knowledge and understanding."** (NKJV/KJV)

Colossians 2:2-3 – "...to the **knowledge of the mystery of God, both of the Father and of Christ, in whom are hidden all the treasures of wisdom and knowledge."**

"God's word makes it clear in Colossians 2:3 that all the treasures of wisdom and knowledge are found in God. James 1:5 tells us that if we lack wisdom, then we should ask God, who gives generously to all without finding fault, and it will be given to us.

So, there is no need for a Christian to find their source of wisdom in any other god or goddess or use another god as an emblem of wisdom, and that's exactly what Delta does" (Pavielle 2024).

ZETA PHI BETA: Bastet

The rituals of Zeta Phi Beta do not directly refer to Bastet. Bastet has been informally associated with the sorority because of the "Cat," and "kittens," some of Zeta's unofficial mascots and symbols. Bastet is the Egyptian goddess (half-cat, half-woman) for women, cats, fertility, and other attributes.

SIGMA GAMMA RHO: Aurora

In Roman mythology, Aurora is the goddess of dawn. She is known to bring forth the beginning of a new day. Prospective SGRho members were part of the Aurora Pledge Club and called Auroras.

IT'S THAT DEEP

OMEGA PSI PHI: 'Shekinah'/Asherah

This is the goddess in Canaanite and Kabbalah (mysticism) spirituality, Merkavah mysticism, and Gnosticism. The rituals refer to Shekinah. The rituals also refer to the 'Spirit of Omega' as female in nature (Out from Among Them Ministries, n.d.).

Kappa Alpha Psi: 1. Apollo 2. Ares

Apollo

Ares

Note. From Wikipedia Commons, CC BY-SA 4.0 <https://creativecommons.org/licenses/by-sa/4.0>, via Wikimedia Commons

Kappa Alpha Psi's foundations have direct links to Greek mythology, especially through founder Elder Watson Diggs' work. "Being a perfectionist, Diggs wanted the ritual and other instruments to be unique and authentic, and himself assumed responsibility for preparing the ceremonial forms. Byron Armstrong was given the job of developing the insignia and emblems. So concerned were they about their assigned duties that one took a course in Greek heraldry and the other studied Greek mythology" (Crump, 1983).

In Greco-Roman mythology, Apollo is known as the god of the sun, music, 'prophecy,' and various other attributes such as healings and plagues. Ares, in Greek mythology is known as the god of war and is briefly included in the initiation ceremony.

For Kappa Alpha Psi, although the god is not mentioned explicitly, Apollo is related to the Altar of Kappa Alpha Psi which is the Sacred Delphic Shrine. This is a false god/deity.

With Apollo's mythological attribute of prophecy, there is also a named high priestess, Pythia, who served as a high priestess at his temple, the Temple of Apollo, by being an oracle for Apollo. As mentioned previously in Section I, God is the One who knows all things. He is the One who counsels and declares what will be. Any oracle, diviner (of 'knowledge'), 'god,' or prophecy outside of the LORD and His Holy Spirit is idolatrous. And if it does not come from God/His kingdom, it comes from the kingdom of darkness.

Partial Repeat from Section I. Rituals - Conflict of an Altar (Continued)

PROCEDURE OF FORMAL MEETINGS

The **Altar** of Kappa Alpha Psi, which is the **Sacred Delphic Shrine**, shall be placed in the center of the room and covered with a crimson and cream coverlet.

The Holy Bible, opened to the Third Chapter of Proverbs shall be placed on the Altar.[21, 22]

What is the Delphic Shrine (as the altar of Kappa Alpha Psi is called the Sacred Delphic Shrine), and what makes it 'sacred'?

Delphi is an ancient city in Greece. It is known for having the Temple of Apollo and the Oracle of Delphi (also named Pythia the high priestess). This was the "most famous ancient oracle, believed to deliver prophecies from the Greek god, Apollo" (Britannica, 2024).

Temple of Apollo, a historical landmark in Greece; also was historically a Panhellenic sanctuary/place of worship

Note. From KufoletoAntonio De Lorenzo and Marina Ventayol, CC BY 3.0 <https://creativecommons.org/licenses/by/3.0>, via Wikimedia Commons

Examples in Ritual of Greek Mythology (paraphrased)[21]

Initiatory Ceremony
"The Thracians are planning to sacrifice this brother to their god Ares and are only willing to grant this brother his liberty if another is sent as replacement for this sacrifice.
After all members volunteered to be sent as a replacement the Lieutenant Strategus prompts the candidate to say that he will die for his brother..."[21]

Tortures
"The candidate is redressed and brought back to **the temple of the Thracian priest**. Only one candle is lit. The candidate is made to lie down on the floor, head towards the altar. The blindfold is removed. Over the candidate stands an executioner with a sword.

The priest enters and inquires whether all is in readiness for **the sacrifice**. He lights a small, red light and calls upon **the god Ares** to show his approval by another red light. However, a blue light is switched on.

All members react horrified and the Lieutenant Strategus cries out that **the gods** show disapproval with the sacrifice.

The Keeper of Records retrieves from the archives of the **sacred scroll** wherein the **high and holy purposes** which **find lodgment in the breast of every loyal member**. The scroll is handed to the candidate to read and **familiarize himself with the Grecian ideals**. He is asked to manifest his fluency in interpreting Grecian scrolls. Unblindfolded, he is unable to read the Greek due to the peculiar arrangement of the text, and, prompted by the Lieutenant Strategus, says so to the Polemarch. The Polemarch sends the candidate to the **Great Oracle of Delphi to obtain the knowledge which he lacks**. He is given a copy of the scroll, blindfolded and sent on his way.[21]

IOTA PHI THETA: Centaur

In Greek mythology, a centaur is a part-human, part-horse creature. Centaurs were known for association with Dionysus (the god of wine), having a weakness for wine and drunkenness, lust, and 'savage,' wild behavior.

Note. From Leonid 2, CC BY-SA 3.0 <https://creativecommons.org/licenses/by-sa/3.0>, via Wikimedia Commons

According to the Epsilon Epsilon Chapter of Iota Phi Theta (n.d.), "Besides **the Fraternity Shield**, the next **most readily identifying symbol of Iota Phi Theta** is **The Centaur**. A Mythical beast with the head and torso of a man, and the body of a stallion, **The Centaur is near and dear to all Men of Iota Phi Theta and its mythology, characteristics, and legacy are a binding force within the Brotherhood**. Additionally, Iota Phi Theta **intakees are referred to as Centaurs**."

PHI BETA SIGMA: Multiple "gods"

"When candidates for admission are first brought in, they are told the traditional story of the original Greek traveler of their fraternity which is as follows: A man was led by the gods to a place called Death Valley to observe the bones of the unfit that did not know the meaning of brotherhood. "He is later taken to the foothills of Mt. Olympus where the greater gods were supposed to live under their ruler Zeus. It was in these mountains that our founding Brothers became Greek. Because they went before you and because you have exemplified the ideals of Brotherhood, Scholarship and Service, YOU are also now part Greek, the process (of becoming Greek) is occurring even as you stand before me" (p. 8 of the ritual book). (During this portion the candidates are in the initiation court with the Sigma Altar, p. 6)" (Rice, 2006).

Rituals

Inferno – Climbing the Mountains
Deputy: Dog, you have come a long journey and have reached the sacred foothills of Mount Olympus in Northeast Greece where **the greater Gods** were supposed to live under their ruler, Zeus. It was in these mountains that one of our founding brothers obtained the bones of an old Greek, brought them back and they have been ground into bone-dust. You have the sacred privilege of now receiving your traditional portion which makes you a Noble Greek of the SIGMA clan. **Open your mouth**, Dog.

Candidate is given about 1 teaspoonful of epsom salts, or substitute - bone dust.[20]

**Refer to 'Food during Rituals' in Section I. Rituals: Altars and Bowing

Inferno – Observing the Wonders of the Mountain

Deputy: Fellow Greek, with your mind's eye you are privileged to observe the wonder of Mt. Olympus where **Aries, the Greek God of War**, resided; **the titan, Prometheus**, stole fire from heaven and taught men its use, for which act **Zeus** punished him by chaining him to the very rock on which you stand.

But SIGMA has outlawed the warring Greeks and is now **under the protection of Pallas Athena, the Goddess of Wisdom, Arts and Industries**. Are you willing to give your time, energy, thought and service to PHI BETA SIGMA? What is your answer?

Candidate answers Yes or No.[20]

III. HYMNS AND CHANTS

PLEDGING AOML (All of My Love)

As mentioned in its definition, a hymn is a religious song or composition that praises God or a god.[6] All 9 NPHC organizations have at least one hymn sung TO the name of the organization, often addressing it as "Thy;" "Thou;" "Thee;" etc. These are just possessive pronouns, meaning "Your" and "You." It causes the organizations to be addressed as an entity. Even as a biblical example, we address God by saying, "Thy will be done." Furthermore, the enemy's agenda is to get the believer to give their praises either to 1) false gods, or 2) simply a thing that is not God. Sure, I know in college and HBCU culture, we have compositions such as an alma mater that also use these pronouns and similar structures; however, please pay attention to the specific words spoken and sung in the following hymns and chants. The themes often prompt members of most of the D9 organizations to profess [all of] their "love, peace, and happiness" to the organizations. Furthermore, there is prompting to pledge "our hearts, our minds," and "strength;" yet God's commandment tells us to love the Lord our God with all our hearts, mind, and strength. You have both God and an organization asking for the same thing (heart, mind, soul, strength, etc.). Who will you choose to be devoted to? God is not pleased with Christ followers saying they are giving "all" of these things (AOML) to another entity. Essentially, it is an attempt of a competition for God's glory. But God is holy, and He will not come second, or be equal, to anything.

Other patterns to take note of are that the organizations are the "pride of our hearts," ascribed glory, seen as the members' delight, and are said to be the way to get into heaven.

***

Upon scanning this QR code, you will find the video content for this Section on Hymns and Chants. The video(s) showcase a rundown of the lyrics, verbatim, as this printed section of the book is summary and critique based. Be sure to follow along with the video content.

ALPHA PHI ALPHA

The Alpha Phi Alpha Hymn
Words by Abram. L. Simpson
Music by John J. Erby; Xi Chapter

Verse 1 says that there is a **bind**ing from **fraternal spirit**.

The *Chorus* acknowledges the organization as being the **pride of their hearts**. Alpha Phi Alpha is addressed as **"thy,"** whose **precepts** are cherished. **A banner is raised** to Alpha Phi Alpha; **glory** and **honor** are also ascribed to "thy."

Verse 2 describes a goal in which **the organization's praises would be sung** (Horner, 2004).

> The Bible says:
> "*I will meditate in* **Thy precepts**..." – Psalms 119:15
> "*But for those who fear You, You have* **raised a banner**..." – Psalms 60:4

The Sphinxman Hymn
This hymn acknowledges the **Mystic Sphinx** and ends with the singers pledging themselves to **obey *its* mandates**.

ALPHA KAPPA ALPHA

Initiation Hymn
Participants [literally] **hail and greet** Alpha Kappa Alpha, addressing Alpha Kappa Alpha both the organization name and **"thee."** Secondly, the hymn states that the sisterhood would be their **delight**. (Remember, a source of delight is a pattern seen in the hymns of multiple organizations).[15]

> *"**Delight** yourself also in the Lord, and He shall give you the desires of your heart." –* Psalms 37:4

Lastly, the hymn expresses that the members will give their **reverence to Alpha Kappa Alpha** forever.[15]

> Reverence is godly fear. *"God is greatly to be feared in the assembly of the saints, and to be held in* **reverence** *by all those around Him." –* Psalms 89:7

The Pledge ('Our Pledge')
To **thee**, O Alpha Kappa Alpha!
We pledge **our hearts, our minds, our strength**:
To foster their teachings,
Obey <u>thy</u> laws,
And make thee Supreme in Service to all mankind O, Alpha Kappa Alpha, We greet thee![15]

> *"You shall love the Lord your God with* **all your heart and mind** *and with all your soul and with* **all your strength** *[your entire being]." –* Deuteronomy 6:5 AMP

> How can you commit your heart, mind/soul, and strength to both God and AKA? (or to 'speak' this?)

<u>*Prayer*</u> <u>from Ritual Book Section IV. Fidelity and Love:</u>
Eternal Spirit, we yearn for a better understanding of **spiritual things** and a **closer walk with Thee**, that we may interpret aright the times in which we live. We long to be able to minister, according to **Thy will**, to People who are troubled and burdened with the cares of the world. Instill into **the hearts of Thy servants** each day, fresh confidence in Thy goodness. Deliver us from fear and worry that we may deal confidently with the fears and worries of others. Strengthen our faith and increase our capacity for sympathy and understanding. Make us glad to bear one another's burdens; and be grateful for opportunities of fulfilling thus the law of eternal life. Amen.[15]

> Again, "Thy;" and who is "Eternal Spirit?" Secondly, this dialogue sounds a lot like the language we profess towards Jesus.

<u>"I Think I Shall Never Know" (Tune of Trees)"</u>
Pg. 5 Ritual Book, 1977

This beginning of this song states that the singer **won't know another love** that thrills her **besides her love for Alpha Kappa Alpha**.[15]

DELTA SIGMA THETA

<u>National Hymn</u>
The verse begins by calling on Delta and then addressing it as "thee." **Praise is given to "thee."**

The chorus continues with singers **rejoicing in "thee"** and pledging loyalty to "thee." It discusses a truth and bond that **purifies the hearts** of the members. As will be discussed in this book's fifth section on Light, this hymn talks of **light of the world**. Lastly, the ideals of the organization are said to be strengthened in the members.[25]

<u>Misc. Delta Chant–</u>
"When you get to heaven and you can't get in, you just show Saint Peter your Delta pin"

> When a believer gets to heaven, it is Jesus they will encounter. May this be a reminder that Jesus is the Way, Truth, and the Life. No one can get to the Father except through Him.

<u>All of My Love Chant</u>
"All of my love, my peace and happiness.. I'm gonna give [it] to Delta"

<u>Pyramid Hymn</u>
Delta is personified in the Chorus as singers ask to hear Delta's voice.

SIGMA GAMMA RHO

> "To **thee ONLY, Sigma Gamma Rho**, I pledge my life, my best efforts, and cooperation. **In thee I pin my faith, hope and trust** so that the order of Sigma Gamma Rho shall be a beacon of light to all womankind who are interested in every phase of education. I therefore dedicate the best that is within me to further its cause" (Anointed Vessel, 2009).

> Psalm 146:3,5 – "Do not **put your trust** in princes, nor in a son of man, in whom there is no help… Happy is he who has the God of Jacob for his help, **whose hope is in the Lord his God**"

> We should only place our faith, hope, and trust in God.

Bow Down (Chant)
This chant states that members will **bow down to the organization**, to the organization's colors, and concludes by acknowledging they **pledged their souls**. (The Mu Beta Chapter of Sigma Gamma Rho Sorority, Inc., n.d.)

In the Beginning (Chant)
This chant describes that **at time of Creation**, there were two people– Eve, a Delta, and Adam, a Que. It goes on to say that KAPsi and SGRho were the ones to fix their mistake. It then says that heaven's streets are the colors rhoyal blue and gold. It concludes by stating **if someone gets to heaven and isn't able to get in, it is because Paul and Peter are Kappas**. (Renee, n.d.)

OMEGA PSI PHI

Omega Dear
The singers tell Omega that they are its own. They express that Omega is their **life** and that they will **sing its praises**. Lastly, the hymn acknowledges Omega's (or "thy") **precepts**; members sing that they will **serve Omega** (or "thee") (Upsilon Omega Chapter, n.d.).

***

KAPPA ALPHA PSI

The Kappa Alpha Psi Hymn
This hymn acknowledges Kappa as the **pride of their hearts** and **source of their delight**. **"Thee"** and **"thy"** are also used in this hymn to address the organization. Similarly to previous hymns of other organizations, singers **sing the praises of Kappa** and **live for Kappa** until they reach the **"Golden Shore"** (Durham (NC) Alumni Chapter, n.d.; Kappa Alpha Nu Journal, 1914)

In regards to the Golden Shore, this fraternity proclaims the "invisible" chapter in which a deceased member is still alive, just invisible and in this realm where the Golden Shore is (Burlington Camden Alumni Chapter, n.d.; https://kappasofburlcam.com/the-chapter-invisible/). This is a biblical contradiction.

The Scrollers Hymn
In the instructions for this hymn, the Scrollers members are told to **bow their heads** each time they mention the Kappa Alpha Psi name. (Gamma Upsilon Chapter, 2015).

Dear Kappa Alpha Psi
This composition describes how the singer **longs and pines for "thee."** It continues to state that the singer/member **walks the path shown by Kappa**. It acknowledges Kappa as one's **guide, strength, joy**, and their own (Gamma Upsilon Chapter, 2015).

The Diamond
By: E. Davidson Hutt

This song describes walking by **ways that are Hellenic**. Secondly, it states that the pin is something they **idolize** ("idolize" is the verbatim word) (Gamma Upsilon Chapter, 2015).

He Rambled
This composition talks of a college student looking to join a fraternity and deciding on Kappa Alpha Psi. He "rambled" until obtaining what is called the **Delphian crown**. It then speaks of the student going back in time and encountering **Noah from the Bible**. The student asked Noah **how he was saved** and Noah's response, according to the song, was **Phi Nu Pi** and admiring the fraternity. Later verses discuss Moses and the Promise Land, how it was **missed because Kappas weren't among the Israelites**. Secondly, it was said that all of the Kappas were in heaven. Lastly, it was said that the student met Satan after his fall; Satan hoped for his own death because **his name was rejected by the fraternity** (Gamma Upsilon Chapter, 2015).

<u>Kappa Alpha Psi March</u>
By: E. Davidson Hutt

This march declares to Kappa that they will continue to **praise its (or "thy") name**. Furthermore, they will **never let its spirit die** (Gamma Upsilon Chapter, 2015).

<u>For Kappa Alpha Psi</u>
By: E. Davidson Hutt

This poem declares to Kappa's clan that they will give their hearts to it ("you") and the bond. Members say they will give their all for the organization. Lastly, it is expressed that there is none like the entity of Kappa (Gamma Upsilon Chapter, 2015).

***

IOTA PHI THETA

<ins>The Hymn of Iota Phi Theta</ins>

Verse 1 addresses Iota Phi Theta and declares that its (**"thy"**) **spirit** is close to **bind the members**. They **glory in the name of Iota Phi Theta**.

In the *Bridge*, singers call unto Iota, **telling Iota to hear them**. Singers tell Iota that they **answer with reverence**.
Lastly, Verse 2 has singers telling Iota that **they bring their hearts**; they make an <ins>eternal</ins> vow (The Hymn of Iota Phi Theta, n.d.).

***

PHI BETA SIGMA

<ins>Crescent Chant</ins>
This chant tells Sigma that they will **raise their hearts through song to Sigma** (or **"thee."**) Through Sigma, their **souls are filled fresh**. The chant ends with declaring that the organization is **the life** (MrGomab60, 2011).

IV. ADDING AND SUBTRACTING FROM THE WORD OF GOD

DO NOT ADD OR TAKE AWAY! God instructs us to not add or take away from His word. Many rituals, hymns, and chants twist and manipulate scripture. Furthermore, these changes to scripture often take God's name or the name of His Word/Law and replace it with the name of the respective organization. Essentially, the organization's rituals alter God's word, drawing glory to the organization itself instead of God.

A second pattern seen throughout these rites is language of the organization being "written on the mind/heart" of its initiates and members. Also (again), the organization is ascribed "all" of one's "love." Adding and subtracting from the Word of God leads to disobedience, and God is by no means pleased.

> *"You shall not add to the word which I command you, nor take from it, that you may keep the commandments of the Lord your God which I command you."* – Deuteronomy 4:2

"For I testify to everyone who hears the words of the prophecy of this book: If anyone adds to these things, God will add to him the plagues that are written in this book; and if anyone takes away from the words of the book of this prophecy, God shall take away his part from the Book of Life, from the holy city, and from the things which are written in this book."

– Revelation 22:18-19

"You shall love the Lord your God with all your heart and mind and with all your soul and with all your strength [your entire being]."

– Deuteronomy 6:5 AMP

How can you commit your heart, mind/soul, and strength to both God and an organization? (or to casually profess this?)

***

ALPHA KAPPA ALPHA

I. Devotion and Promise (pg. 24-25)

Basileus: Let us pray. Repeat after me:

Open then my eyes, O God, that I may behold the wondrous works <u>of this great organization</u>. Make me to understand the ideals and purposes of this sisterhood so that I may continue the great work so nobly begun. Take from me any selfishness and lack of purpose which could keep me from following the ideals of the organization. Awaken within me holy desires, **inspire me with a new enthusiasm of the <u>revered FOUNDERS</u>** and grant me wisdom and strength that I may render service to all mankind. In Jesus' name I pray. Amen.[15]

This prayer in the initiation ritual altered and subtracted from Scripture by replacing [God's] "Your/Thy law" with "works of this great organization."

Psalms 119:18 – ***"Open thou mine eyes, that I may behold wondrous things out of thy law."*** (KJV/NKJV)

IV. Fidelity and Love (pg. 32)
Candidates <u>kneel</u> and take the following oaths.
I, _____ (Name), do solemnly promise always to live up to the ideals of the organization, to stand by Alpha Kappa Alpha in every undertaking, to render assistance to any soror at all times, and to refrain from any expression of ill-will. I shall keep in my heart these words: **"Set a guard over my mouth: keep watch over the door of my lips."**[15]

Original Scripture, spoken to God:
Psalms 141:3 – *"Set a guard, O Lord, over my mouth; keep watch over the door of my lips."*

DELTA SIGMA THETA

"THE GREATEST OF THESE" – A Meditation for Delta
(A paraphrase of 1 Corinthians 13)
by Dorothy I. Height

A few quotes from the Meditation –
"…..and though I prophesy, **know all Delta laws, Ritual, traditions and secrets, and can recite them glibly**;
And though I have such absolute devotion to duty that I can do
Anything my hands undertake, and have not love, I am nothing….

….strive with all my might for Delta,
And have no love, I make it amount to nothing.

A true Soror is very patient, very kind.
Her love for her Sorors knows no jealousy; she makes no parade…
A true Delta is never glad when others go wrong….

…As for interpreting the law, it will be superseded; as for tongues,
They will cease; **as for a college education, it will be superseded**.
For now we know only bit by bit and we prophesy bit by bit;
But **when the true sisterly spirit is attained, the uncharitable shall fade away. When I was a pyramid, I talked as a Pyramid, I understood as a Pyramid, I thought as a Pyramid,**
But now that I have become a Delta,
I am done with the ways of those intending to be Deltas.

At present we see only the great potentialities
Of a Sisterhood founded on Christian principles…

...Thus faith, and hope and love last on, these three, but in Delta Sigma Theta, the greatest of these is love."

(The Official Ritual of the Grand Chapter of Delta Sigma Theta Sorority, Inc., p.79-80, 1996)

"Though I speak with the tongues of men and of angels, but have not love, I have become sounding brass or a clanging cymbal. And though I have the gift of prophecy, and understand all mysteries and all knowledge, and though I have all faith, so that I could remove mountains, but have not love, I am nothing. And though I bestow all my goods to feed the poor, and though I give my body to be burned, but have not love, it profits me nothing. **Love suffers long and is kind**; *love does not envy; love does not parade itself, is not puffed up; does not behave rudely, does not seek its own, is not provoked, thinks no evil; does not rejoice in iniquity, but rejoices in the truth; bears all things, believes all things, hopes all things, endures all things. Love never fails. But whether there are prophecies, they will fail; whether there are tongues, they will cease; whether there is knowledge, it will vanish away. For we know in part and we prophesy in part.* **But when that which is perfect has come, then that which is in part will be done away. When I was a child, I spoke as a child, I understood as a child, I thought as a child; but when I became a man, I put away childish things. For now we see in a mirror, dimly, but then face to face.** *Now I know in part, but then I shall know just as I also am known.* **And now abide faith, hope, love, these three; but the greatest of these is love.** *"*

– 1 Corinthians 13:1-13

ZETA PHI BETA

Basileus: Zeta has been written upon your hearts and minds. You are now ready to receive the light of Zeta.
Each candidate lights her candle from the one on the table.
Basileus: This candle represents the light of Zeta which is to ever keep burning within your hearts.[17]

PHI BETA SIGMA

Inferno – Observing the Wonders of the Mountain
Deputy: Fellow Greek, SIGMA has been written on your breast; would that it could be **written on your heart**. Ah! It must be! It must be!
Snatch off the adhesive tape.
Deputy: SIGMA did not come off. It cannot come off. It is there to stay. **It is upon your heart** and there **it will remain until your heart ceases to throb**.[20]

V. LIGHT

CLAIMS OF 'THE LIGHT;' ONLY JESUS IS THE LIGHT OF THE WORLD

Many of the organizations claim to have 'the light,' to be 'the light of the world,' or to bring the 'light of life.' This is blasphemous. Only **Jesus Christ** is the light of the world and the light of life. **He is the only light**, and **the only Way** to come out of darkness and into light.

> *"Then Jesus spoke to them again, saying, "I am the light of the world. He who follows Me shall not walk in darkness, but have the light of life."*
> – John 8:12

> *"In Him was life, and the life was the light of men."* – John 1:4

> *"Satan disguises himself as an angel of light."* – 2 Corinthians 11:14 – (no wonder so many ancient philosophies, religions, and doctrines claim to have light.)

This concept of light did not begin with collegiate fraternities and sororities either. Even in Freemasonry, there is said to be a symbolic use of 'light' in their rituals and ceremonies. It is also said that the Freemasonry initiates come out of darkness, into the light, when they come into knowledge of the Masonic teachings and rites. Light, "it is not only the first symbol that is ceremonially introduced to the initiate, but continues all through his progress in the Craft. Truth and Wisdom constitute part of light, which pervades the whole basis of Freemasonry to the extent that Freemasons are even called the Sons of Light. In the First Degree alone the word is introduced to the candidate in three different perspectives. Those perspectives being, the material light, or the lesser lights, the emblematic light or the Volume of the Sacred Law, and the spiritual light or the creative will of the Supreme Being. These concepts and others that follow after the First Degree are amply enshrouded in illuminating phraseology remembered by every Freemason. Their full import may not be perceived by all but they are constantly there in the rituals of our ceremonies" (Grand Lodge of Ancient, Free & Accepted Masons of Oregon Washington Masonic Lodge No. 46 A. F. & A. M., 2017).

***

ALPHA PHI ALPHA

Section 15.

BROUGHT TO LIGHT. All members shall say: "BEHOLD! BEHOLD!" as the candidate's blindfold is withdrawn, and he sees **"ALPHA PHI ALPHA, THE LIGHT OF THE WORLD"** in large letters just over the **altar**.[14]

ALPHA KAPPA ALPHA

"I See the Light" (chant)
This chant discusses how the member(s) see the **light** and only a **few can obtain it** (1st Step Media, 2018).

DELTA SIGMA THETA

(from Hymn section)
Delta's National Hymn describes Delta Sigma Theta **lighting the world**.[25]

ZETA PHI BETA

Basileus: You are now ready to receive **the light of Zeta**.
Each candidate lights her candle from the one on the table.
Basileus: This candle represents **the light of Zeta** which is to ever keep burning within your hearts.[17]

Charge
The Basileus or an assigned soror: I charge you to go forth holding high **the light of Zeta** that the world might know that you are a Zeta.[17]

SIGMA GAMMA RHO

> p.R4-R5 of the Ritual Book– "…In thee I pin my faith, hope and trust so that the order of **Sigma Gamma Rho shall be a beacon of light to all womankind** who are interested in every phase of education…" (Rice, 2006)

OMEGA PSI PHI

> *Fifth Test*
> *Basileus:* Whence come ye, my friends clothed as ye be and accompanied by these my true and tried brothers?
> *Neophyte Commandant:* From the outer chamber of darkness into **the Shekinah of light of Omega.**
>
> On bringing you from the darkness of selfish and self-centered lives **into the fullness and light of life in Omega**…[19]
>
> *Language of the Pin*
> The Greek lamp signifies our endeavors in dark places ever illuminated by **the mystical light of Omega**.[19]

IOTA PHI THETA

<u>The Ceremony (The Centaur Ceremony)</u>
    E) The **Centaurs** should be made to hold Yellow Candles to signify that '**BROTHERHOOD IS THE <u>LIGHT OF THE WORLD</u>.**'[29]

PHI BETA SIGMA

    "The Sigma Light" was published by J. Edgar Smith and Frances Hall. It is not a ritual but an authored writing and concept. This light is thought to provide guidance to men who want to join the organization.

VI. SPIRITUAL BINDING

BEING BOUND/YOKED

The language in many of the rituals declare that the initiate is bound either to the organization, to the vows and oaths being spoken, to higher 'forces' and 'authorities,' and to the other individuals in the organization worldwide. When you consider the spiritual implications discussed in this book thus far, this 'binding' goes far beyond simply a "serious commitment" to serve in the organization. Your **agreement** is what allows a demonic spirit or principality to access your soul or bloodline even. Satan knows that unless he can get you to agree to a thing, then he cannot put these covenants or bondages upon you. Furthermore, when you willingly agree/bind to a demonic covenant, it conflicts with the covenant you have with God. Especially, but not exclusively, by saying "I do," "I will," "I am," or "I submit," in these rituals and declarations, you have agreed to a binding that is spiritual.

    This is language we use in the covenant of marriage— to spouses and Christ. Marriage is binding. Secondly, it is not ideal to be so closely knit with people who are unbelievers. The organizations accept membership of people from any religious background (or none at all). Prospective members are not asked if they are saved or Christian or not. But let's say one's direct line or chapter was full of Christian individuals; what about the members nationally and internationally that are bound together as well? The idea is that the ties go beyond an individual chapter, but ALL a part of that organization are seen as brothers and sisters, in the rituals as well.

For example, from Omega Psi Phi's ritual, "you are about to take upon yourself an oath which will **bond you most intimately to every brother of the Omega Psi Phi Fraternity.**"[19] The introduction to Alpha Kappa Alpha's ritual states, "There is still another **bond** which many believe to be our strongest link–**the vows which are made by each member** of our Sorority. These solemn promises not only bind us to one another, but also to a common goal."[15] Ritually, most of the organizations declare that there is a binding in fellowship. Remember, we are commanded to not be unequally yoked together with unbelievers. Light cannot mix with darkness, and bad company **corrupts** good morals. We do not want to grieve the Holy Spirit by using our temples to bind with darkness. We are further commanded to **come out from among them and be separate.**

> 2 Corinthians 6:12-18 –
> *You are not restricted by us, but* ***you are restricted by your own affections.*** *Now in return for the same (I speak as to children),* ***you also be open.***
>
> ***Do not be unequally yoked together with unbelievers.*** *For what **fellowship** has **righteousness with lawlessness**? And what **communion** has **light with darkness**? And what accord has Christ with Belial? Or what part has a **believer with an unbeliever**? And what **agreement** has the **temple of God with idols**? For you are the temple of the living God.*
>
> *As God has said:*
>
> *"I will dwell in them*
> *And walk among them.*
> *I will be their God,*
> *And they shall be My people."*

Therefore
**"Come out from among them
And be separate, says the Lord.
Do not touch what is unclean,
And I will receive you."**
*"I will be a Father to you,
And you shall be My sons and daughters,
Says the LORD Almighty."*

Revelation 18:4 – **"And I heard another voice from heaven saying, 'Come out of her, my people, lest you share in her sins…"**

Isaiah 52:11 – **"Depart! Depart! Go out from there, touch no unclean thing; go out from the midst of her, be clean, you who bear vessels of the LORD."**

Psalms 86:10-12 – **"For You are great, and do wondrous things; You alone are God. Teach me Your way, O Lord; I will walk in Your truth; UNITE my heart to fear Your name."**

***

ALPHA KAPPA ALPHA

Introduction
There is still another bond which many believe to be our strongest link–the vows which are made by each member of our

Sorority. These solemn promises not only bind us to one another, but also to a common goal.[15]

II. Obedience (pg. 27-28)
Basileus to Candidate: Are you willing to be **submissive** and **in every way to subjugate yourself** to the **highest authority**?
Pilot to Candidates: Repeat after me: "I Am." Candidates: I am.
Basileus: What proof have you.
Pilot to Candidates: Repeat after me: **"I show my submission by kneeling."**
Candidates kneel a few minutes.[15]

> Definition of **subjugate**
> ➢ [to] bring under domination or control, especially by conquest[26]

This is a binding through submission...

IV. (After) Fidelity and Love (pg. 33)
Basileus: May you always remember that you are not only joining with individuals but you are uniting with the Alpha Kappa Alpha.

Basileus: You are entering the last phase of this sacred hour, and are about to join hands with those Alpha Kappa Alpha women who continually remind themselves of the pledge they made and the loyalties they owe. May you always remember that you are not only joining with individuals but you are uniting with the Alpha Kappa Alpha. May you also become increasingly aware that the pledges and the vows which you have made before God and in the presence of Alpha Kappa Alpha women here assembled...[15]

DELTA SIGMA THETA

<u>The Crossing-Over Ceremony</u> (pg. 181)
Step 6: I take the sixth step and promise to embrace all Deltas everywhere as my sisters.[16]

<u>The Initiation Ceremony</u> (pg. 187 - 189)
President: The **bonding** of new members is a **sacred obligation** which we **share** with the **Deltas throughout the world**… As Sorors we now take up our solemn obligation to **bond** qualified **Candidates to <u>commitments from which they may never be freed</u>.**

President: Now **you are about to take upon yourself vows and obligations from which you can never be freed. <u>They will follow you to the final judgment</u>.** Before we proceed further in this ceremony, I shall ask each of you by name to affirm that you of **your own free will** and accord seek admission into Delta Sigma Theta Sorority by **saying "I do."**

(The President shall ask each Candidate by name to affirm her decision by saying I do.)[16]

(1969 edition)
President: As we proceed in this ceremony will each of you pause to consider this question: "Do you of your own free will and accord seek admission into Delta Sigma Theta Sorority?"
Candidates: I do.
President: You seek of your own free will admission to our sisterhood and we agree to accept you. **You are about to take upon yourselves vows and obligations from which you can never be freed. They will follow you to the Final Judgment.** I charge you that you approach with serious minds as we do now

IT'S THAT DEEP

proceed.[25]

Beta Hymn
(last stanza)

This hymn describes the Delta Sigma Theta members being **bonded through devotion**. It declares that their bond will stand even if they are **scattered**. It ends by saying nothing should break their **ties**.

ZETA PHI BETA

Basileus: We are a group of college women organized as a sister Greek-letter organization to **Phi Beta Sigma Fraternity**, do hereby **bind ourselves together** for the purpose of promoting the cause of education by encouraging the highest standards of scholarship through scientific, literary, cultural, and educational programs…[17]

> Zeta Phi Beta and Phi Beta Sigma Fraternity are constitutionally bound as brother and sister organizations. This translates to spiritual binding as well.

Funeral Services
During the burial service of a soror, members join hands in a circle and sing a hymn in which "Christian love" is replaced by **"Zeta love"** from the original hymn written by preacher John Fawcett in 1782: "Blest be the tie that **binds our hearts in Christian love**; the fellowship of kindred minds is like to that above."

69

SIGMA GAMMA RHO

Sister's Keeper Chant/Song
This song describes how the sisters are all **One**; they do everything together, such as to stay, win, lose and die all together. It also describes that the sisters do what their sisters do. What one's sister knows, she too knows. What one's sister doesn't know, she also doesn't know (Horntip, 2001).

Sigma Gamma Rho Hymn
The singers of this hymn profess to sing to Sigma Gamma Rho forever. Also sung is that members are bound through ties. It ends by expressing that Sigma Gamma Rho's name is worthy (Smithsonian, 2017).

OMEGA PSI PHI

The first Neophyte having been brought into the Oath Chamber, the District Representative shall proceed to talk on the value, sacredness and significance of the oath. The District Representative recites: My friends, we are now about to go through the most sacred part of the entire initiation; **you are about to take upon yourself an oath which will bond you most intimately to every brother of the Omega Psi Phi Fraternity,** and enlist you in a cause with which you will at all times be expected to sympathize, whose principles you will uphold and defend, whose name you will honor, and to which you will give your full support. Think well of what you are doing;

think of the responsibility you are taking upon yourself, and of your obligation to the Fraternity.

The taking of this oath is not a matter of mere formality, but a far more **serious transaction**. It is **the centralizing of all the higher forces** within one upon a great principle in the presence of Almighty God, the keeping of which immediately decides the man.

I further promise and swear that I will support the Constitution of the Omega Psi Phi Fraternity, maintain its standards, and never prove traitor to any trust imposed in me by the Omega Psi Fraternity; **binding myself** under no less a penalty if I forsake thee, O Omega, than to have my right hand lose her cunning and my tongue cleave to the roof of my mouth. So help me God, and keep me faithful and steadfast to the end of life's journey.[19]

Language of the Pin
...Across the center of the Pin shall be inscribed the three Greek letters, Omega Psi Phi, above which there shall be a star and below which there shall be a Greek lamp. This pin speaks in a language peculiar to Omega; **the three Greek letters bespeak the linking of souls as evidenced by the friendship of David and Jonathan...**[19]

KAPPA ALPHA PSI

Unsourced (due to a missing citation from my initial research), there is documentation of initiates being told that their oath is the step that leads them to being **bound to the hearts of**

thousands of other **Kappas**.

Secondly, member Dr. Samuel D. Proctor stated, "I am still amazed that ten young men studying here at Indiana years ago, could conceive of an idea so **thoroughly rooted and grounded** in concrete reality that it would sweep through the decades for a half century, gathering momentum, capturing the imagination and the enthusiasm of thousands of young men, congealing into **a fellowship that binds together from the far corners of this great nation**" (Crump, 1983).

PHI BETA SIGMA

Pre-Initiation Preparations: This is the meeting when **the Soul, the being, the complete entity of Sigma**, along with its secrets, will be **infused into new brothers**.[20]

Ritual book pg. 10 states that the fraternity "is a **spiritual fellowship that binds us in all** activities along life's **narrow pathway**" (Rice, 2006)

Initiation Ceremony
Chief Justice to the candidates: Cometh thou hither of **thy own free will** and accord to be initiated into the mysteries and secrets of this fraternity.
Deputy, telling the candidates to answer: Say, I do.
Candidates answer: **I do**[20]

Inferno – Observing the Wonders of the Mountain
Deputy: Fellow Greek, SIGMA has been written on your breast; would that it could be written on your heart. Ah! It must be! It

must be!

Snatch off the adhesive tape.

Deputy: **SIGMA did not come off. It cannot come off. It is there to stay. It is upon your heart and there it will remain until your heart ceases to throb.**

The ideals of our fraternity…

It is a **spiritual fellowship that binds** us in all activities along life's narrow pathway.

These exercises which you are passing through were not provided for the entertainment of those who are to be your brothers, but to impress upon you the seriousness of your new relationship. You must keep ever burning on your heart the Essence of this Initiation and ever remember that **we are bound together by a triple cord** of love in Brotherhood, Service and Scholarship.[20]

A Biblical Outlook on Pronouncing Vows

Numbers Chapter 30 is a great chapter to help us understand how the Lord regards vows. Vows and oaths must be carefully kept; it is seen as being bound by an agreement.

> vs. 2 – *"If a man makes a vow to the Lord, or swears an oath to bind himself by some agreement, he shall not break his word; he shall do according to all that proceeds out of his mouth."*

Secondly, on vows, people who publicly denounce and renounce their previous organizations have often been criticized. People ask, "What's the point of announcing that you are leaving the organization?" For one, the Word tells us to expose the deeds of darkness. Not only do we overcome by the word of our testimony, but public sharing helps another Believer to be set free from their bondage. However, on the topic of vows, there is scriptural reason for public denouncing and renouncing.

> Leviticus 5:4-5 – *"Or if a person swears, speaking thoughtlessly with his lips to do evil or to do good,* **whatever it is that a man may pronounce by an oath**, *and he is unaware of it - when he realizes it, then he shall be guilty in any of these matters. And it shall be, when he is guilty in any of these matters, that* **he shall confess that he has sinned in that thing.**"

There is so much power in confessing, repenting, and public testifying. God is merciful and truly a Light in dark places.

VII. CONCLUDING THOUGHTS

1. THINGS THAT CONTRADICT SCRIPTURE AND/OR ARE DEMONIC;
2. WITCHCRAFT, PAGAN AND OCCULT PRACTICES;
3. SECRETS ONLY BELONG TO THE LORD

---

1. Things that Contradict Scripture and/or are Demonic

ALPHA KAPPA ALPHA

Ritual: IV. Fidelity and Love
(As also mentioned in Section III. Hymns and Chants)

Prayer: **Eternal Spirit**, we yearn for a better understanding of **spiritual things** and a **closer walk with Thee**, that we may interpret aright the times in which we live. We long to be able to minister, according to **Thy will**, to People who are troubled and burdened with the cares of the world. **Instill into the hearts of Thy servants** each day, fresh confidence in Thy goodness…[15]

> *As asked previously, who is "Eternal Spirit?" This dialogue sounds a lot like the language we profess towards Jesus. The spiritual conflict here is that an 'Eternal Spirit' and 'spiritual things' are mentioned, but Jesus Christ and/or the Holy Spirit is not mentioned. As a Christian, you don't want to invoke or welcome any spirit except the spirit of our God, for any spirit outside of His is demonic.*

DELTA SIGMA THETA

Part of DST Candidate Syllabus:
"A woman who becomes a Candidate is **under the shadow of Minerva**, and in no way could we offend one who is **under her grace!**"

> (Delta Sigma Theta Sorority, INC., GRAND CHAPTER, CANDIDATE SYLLABUS, 1987-1990, p. 38)

> *A child of God should only be under the shadow of the Almighty and under the grace of covenant with Him.*

>> Psalms 91:1 – *"He who dwells in the secret place of the Most High shall abide under the shadow of the Almighty."*

>> Romans 6:14 – *"For sin shall not have dominion over you, for you are not under law but under grace."*

IT'S THAT DEEP

(Following "Delta Prayer"):
President: We believe in **a spiritual life** but we leave to **the individual** the selection of **the medium for its outward manifestation.**

A fire—mist and a planet
A **crystal ball** and a cell,
A jellyfish and a saurian,
And caves where cavemen dwell—
The a sense of law and beauty
And a face turned from the clod,
Some of us call it evolution, and others call it God.
A haze on the far horizon,
The infinite tender sky,
The ripe, rich tint of the cornfields,
And the wild goose sailing high—
And all over the upland and lowland
The charm of the goldenrod,
Some of us call it Autumn, and others call it God.
Like the tides on a crescent sea beach,
When the moon is new and thin,
Into our hearts high yearnings,
Come rolling and surging in—
Come from the mystic ocean
Whose rim no foot has trod,
Some of us call it longing, and **others call it God**.
A picket frozen on duty,
A mother starved for her brood,
Socrates drinking the hemlock,
And Jesus on the rood—
And millions who, humble and nameless
The straight hard pathway trod,
Some call it consecration, and others call it God.[25]

This is <u>syncretism</u>, just as in Freemasonry, where various religions and spiritual beliefs are welcomed and merged. Furthermore, this passage is a poem written by William Herbert Carruth called "Each in His Own Tongue" (Carruth, 1909). It explores the various interpretations of the divine. It highlights that there are multiple experiences and beliefs regarding religion, philosophy, and science. Use of this poem, in this spiritual context, reiterates the belief in leaving to the individual their expression and manifestation of spirituality.

(1969)

Candidate: I, __(Name)__, do promise **in the presence of the Eternal Spirit of Truth**, and these finite witnesses, that I will never reveal in any manner whatsoever, for any purpose whatsoever, any of the secrets, passwords, signs, grips, or other confidences entrusted to my keeping as a member of Delta Sigma Theta Sorority, now at the time of my initiation into the sisterhood, or that may hereafter from time to time be so entrusted. I do further solemnly promise that I will dedicate my life to the nine cardinal virtues of Delta Sigma Theta. This pledge is upon my sacred word of honor.[25]

Who/what exactly is the "Eternal Spirit of Truth?" Jesus' or the Holy Spirit's names are not named near here. The Bible says in John 15:26 that the Holy Spirit is the Spirit of truth, **"but when the Helper comes, whom I shall send to you from the Father, the Spirit of truth who proceeds from the Father, He will testify of Me."**

The Pyramid Induction Ceremony (pg. 118)

Keeper of the Muses and the Graces: I am the Keeper of the Muses and the Graces. Recognizing the importance of music, dance and all the arts in our lives, I bring aesthetic spirit to inspire our efforts. Our African ancestors brought dance and music into all their rituals and rites of passage. The Greeks summoned the Muses and the Graces to enliven all special occasions. I am responsible for integrating music, dance, and all other art forms into the initiation process.[16]

> In Greek Mythology, the Muses and Graces were goddesses, known to be daughters of Zeus. They indeed were also known for the arts, such as poetry, dance, and music. Here again, we have the involvement and association of deity mythology. Secondly, African rituals and rites are also acknowledged here. Not all of our African ancestors used dance and music for Christian or secular purposes.

Day 1: The Jewel Ceremony | Compassion (for Pyramids)

Assisting Soror #1: To acknowledge our **ancestors** means we are aware that we did not make ourselves. Let us be reminded always that we are not the first to suffer, rebel, fight, love and die. The grace with which we embrace life, in spite of the pain, the sorrow, is always a measure of what has gone before.

Jewel Compassion: Sorors and Pyramids, let us lovingly call the roll of our Delta Sigma Theta ancestors. Please stand. Let us recite the Founders names as a **mantra**[16]

Definition of **mantra**

> - a mystical formula of invocation or incantation (as in Hinduism)[27]
> - (originally in Hinduism and Buddhism) a word or sound repeated to aid concentration in meditation.
>   > "a mantra is given to a trainee meditator when his teacher initiates him"[28]

Not only are mantras used in New Age spirituality and eastern meditative religions such as Hinduism and Buddhism, but the mantra in this ceremony is an incantation upon the name of the Delta ancestors. Many spiritualities outside of Christianity have veneration of ancestors.

Day 8: The Jewel Ceremony | Purity (for Pyramids)
Assisting Soror #9: …**You are a child of the universe**, no less than the trees and the stars; you have a right to be here. And whether or not it is clear to you, no doubt the universe is unfolding as it should.
Therefore, be at peace with **GOD, whatever you conceive Him to be.** And whatever your labor and aspiration, in the noisy confusion of life keep peace with your soul.
With all its sham, drudgery and broken dreams, it is still a beautiful world. Be cheerful. Strive to be happy.[16]

> (from a poem called Desiderata by Max Ehrmann, 1927)

As just previously mentioned, this too is syncretism.

OMEGA PSI PHI

The taking of this oath is not a matter of mere formality, but a far more **serious transaction**. It is the **centralizing of all the higher forces within one** upon a great principle in the presence of Almighty God, the keeping of which immediately decides the man.

Are you willing to take upon yourself this obligation? *Answer yes or no.*[19]

KAPPA ALPHA PSI

Opening Ceremony
ACHIEVEMENT.
...and pledge ourselves to encourage among us a Spirit of Fraternity, a broad and **comprehensive knowledge of the phenomena and forces of the universe**...[21]

> Seeking knowledge of forces of the universe has nothing to do with the Living God. Outside of scientific facts, attributing knowledge or power to the "Universe" is spirituality and in contradiction to scripture.
> Habakkuk 2:14 – "For the earth will be filled with the knowledge of the glory of the Lord, as the waters cover the sea."

"Tortures" Section
The candidate is set free and sent home.... He is admitted and after a welcome by the Polemarch, seated to determine whether

he is fit to **share the glory** and privileges of a member of **Kappa Alpha Psi**.[21]

To share the glory of Kappa Alpha Psi denotes that Kappa Alpha Psi has glory, and a glory that is shared. A believer should not seek to receive shared glory from their organization. In Isaiah 42:8, God says **"I am the Lord, that is My name; and My glory I will not give to another, nor My praise to carved images."** In previous sections of this book, it is displayed how carved images, praise, and glory is attributed to Kappa Alpha Psi and the spiritual associations. Therefore, this text in the ritual is in contradiction with God's Word.

IOTA PHI THETA

<u>Going On Ceremony</u>
Polaris: ...I ask for the Chaplain to **invoke the presence of our God(s) to oversee** our Mission...
Chaplain: **"Amen."** (Brothers should be aware and be respectful of the **various religions and/or beliefs by the various Brothers** of the Chapter)[29]

Polaris: ...no great undertaking has been done without the aid of prayer. Young men, **kneel and pray <u>together</u>** that **your God(s) <u>will watch over you and guide you along the way</u>**.[29]

Just as previously mentioned in this Section with the Delta ritual, this is syncretism, again as in Freemasonry where various religions and spiritual beliefs are welcomed and merged. With the words of this specific ceremony, the **presence of other gods is literally invoked.** Saying "amen" is even to come into agreement. This is an unequal yoking and partaking with demons. If there is a spirit invoked that is not the Holy Spirit/from Yahweh, the only other source it could come from is Satan's kingdom. This is also the opposite of being set apart as the brothers are being made "aware," (and are welcoming, rather) the beliefs and gods of their various brothers. As the other brothers kneel and pray for their gods to watch over and guide them, those 'gods' (spirits) are also involving themselves in the life of the Believer brother.

It is one thing to be respectful of those who have different beliefs or religions; it is another thing to agree with and invoke the presence of the spirits of their gods.

PHI BETA SIGMA

Inferno – Observing the Wonders of the Mountain
…The assistant deputies and Dr. Luke take a piece of ice or dull instrument and go through the process of **carving PHI BETA SIGMA** *on the breast of each of the candidates.*
Deputy: Dr. Luke, draw some of this embryo Greek's blood by **carving Sigma** above his heart.

> Exodus 20:3-4 – *"You shall have no other gods before Me. You shall not make for yourself a **carved image**–any likeness of anything that is in heaven above, or that is in the earth beneath, or that is in the water under the earth"*

Since branding is illegal, by force, a piece of ice or any dull instrument is used to carve the Greek letter sigma outline on candidate's chest. Then, place a

piece of adhesive tape over the spot.
Deputy: Fellow Greek, SIGMA has been written on your breast; would that it could be **written on your heart**. Ah! It must be! It must be!
Snatch off the adhesive tape.
Deputy: SIGMA did not come off. It cannot come off. It is there to stay. It is **upon your heart** and there it will remain **until your heart ceases to throb.**[20]

(Meaning of Figures on the Seal)
The **dove represents the fraternity** as a <u>**messenger of peace and goodwill**</u> to all mankind.[20]

> The dove is actually a representation of the Holy Spirit. *"And the Holy Spirit descended in bodily form like a **dove** upon Him." –* Luke 3:22

> Secondly, verbatim in scripture, Jesus Christ was and is the messenger of peace and goodwill to all mankind.

> When Jesus was born, *"the angel said unto them, Fear not: for, behold, I bring you good tidings of great joy, which shall be* **to all people**. *For unto you is born this day in the city of David a Saviour, which is Christ the Lord… And suddenly there was with the angel a multitude of the heavenly host praising God, and saying, Glory to God in the highest, and on earth* **peace, good will toward men.**" – Luke 2:10-11, 13-14 (KJV)

IT'S THAT DEEP

INVICTUS by William Ernest Henley (1875)

>Not all chapters require their initiates to recite "Invictus" by William Ernest Henley during their intake processes, but many do, especially the ones that pledge underground. The poem is below.

Out of the night that covers me,
  Black as the pit from pole to pole,
I thank **whatever gods** may be
  For my **unconquerable soul**.

In the fell clutch of circumstance
  I have not winced nor cried aloud.
Under the bludgeonings of chance
  My head is bloody, but unbowed.

Beyond this place of wrath and tears
  Looms but the Horror of the shade,
And yet the menace of the years
  Finds and shall find me unafraid.

It matters not how strait the gate,
  How charged with punishments the scroll,
I am the master of my fate,
  I am the captain of my soul.

The first issue here is, "<u>I thank whatever gods may be.</u>" This already violates the first of the 10 Commandments, that "you shall have no other gods before Me."

Invictus is a poem with a theme of resilience and overcoming adversity. Its title comes from a Latin word that means 'unconquerable' or 'undefeated,' hence the ending of the first stanza that says, "For my unconquerable soul."

This poem, although motivational, idolizes man, more so as if man is invincible. I will explain that a bit further. It says that you have control over your own life; you guide your future and soul. This is the next issue; man is not invincible. Man needs God, the One with true power. Lastly, the third stanza mentions, "It matters not how strait the gate…" "I am the master of my fate; I am the captain of my soul." Frankly, it matters how strait the gate is. God says the gate is very strait, and there are few who find it. The definition of "strait" is a place that is narrow, cramped, and of limited spatial capacity. This narrow gate is what leads to life. Without finding it, and having God, man's fate is simply destruction. God is the Master of our fate, both in this earthly life and in eternity. Check out this scripture on fate, and the following scriptures as well.

Proverbs 19:21 – *"Many plans are in a person's heart, but the Lord's decree will prevail."* (CSB)

Matthew 7:13-14 – *"Enter by the narrow gate; for wide is the gate and broad is the way that leads to destruction, and there are many who go in by it. Because narrow is the gate and difficult is the way which leads to life, and there are few who find it."*

Matthew 7:14 – *"…because strait is the gate, and narrow is the way, which leadeth unto life…"* (KJV)

Exodus 20:3 – *"You shall have no other gods before Me."*

***

2. Witchcraft, Pagan and Occult Practices

During the initiation ceremonies of many of the organizations, initiates are told to gather in a circle, sometimes a semi-circle. Ex-members recall parts of their initiation where they joined in a circle with their fellow initiates. It was brought to my remembrance that witches purposely gather in circles. I wondered if this practice was at all related to fraternal rites.

Through researching Wicca (modern paganism, witchcraft, and Western esotericism), I found that witches have a practice of 'casting a circle.' Articles on circle casting DIRECTLY state that circle casting is intended for RITUALS. So, when you see that initiates in these organizations are standing in a circle, likely holding hands, for their RITUAL, more questions arise. As a side note, in Wicca, there is usually a 'high priest' standing in the middle of the circle. High priests in those practices are simply leaders of the group or coven. During the Deltas' ritual, the Leader of the Minerva Circle (LMC) stands in the middle of the circle formed. I mention this to shed light to the practices that are subtly introduced in these rituals.

What is the purpose of circle casting in witchcraft?

> Casting a circle is seen as a magic technique and an art. Its purposes include 'centering energy' and invoking spirits within the circle (witches will literally 'call on' the spirits they want to invoke. Investigate what rituals and words are used during circle formations of D9 initiation rituals). There is a common practice of forming the circle, using a candle (known as a 'ritual tool') within the circle, and verbally setting intentions, meditations, or prayers (Art of the Root, 2023).

Quotes from an Article on Casting a Circle for a Ritual/Spellwork:

> "In modern Paganism, one of the facets common to many traditions is the use of a circle as a sacred space. While other religions rely on the use of a building such as a church or a temple to hold worship, Wiccans and Pagans can cast a circle pretty much any place they choose. This is particularly handy on those pleasant summer evenings when you decide to hold ritual out in the back yard under a tree instead of in your living room!" (Wigington, 2018).

> "Figure out where your Circle should be cast. In some traditions, a Circle is physically marked on the ground, while in others it is merely visualized by each member of the group. If you have an indoor ritual space, you can mark the Circle on the carpet. Do whichever your tradition calls for. Once the Circle is designated, it is usually navigated by the High Priest or High Priestess, holding an athame, a candle, or a censer"
> (Wigington, 2018).

Quotes on being a High Priest(ess):

> "Many Wiccan traditions have a specific training program for members of the priesthood. They require initiation to the Third Degree for a person to become a High Priestess or High Priest.
>
> As to what a High Priest(ess) does, the most obvious duty is conducting sabbats and esbats. That is to say, they lead the ritual within the sacred circle. That's the least of what they do, though, as they are the administrative officers of the coven, the teachers, and the advisors for the members and students" (Tarrant, 2019).

To expound on my point of the subtle introductions

of witchcraft practices, be mindful of any experiences where a leader of the chapter, such as the LMC for example, leads the rituals in a circle similarly to a Wiccan high priest. Also, be mindful that there are degrees and ranks in witchcraft, Freemasonry, and in secret societies as well. In Greek organizations specifically, there are ranks when someone surpasses their first term or year as a neophyte and becomes a prophyte.

Lastly, in casting a circle, the one doing the initiation can choose to stand in the center of the circle once it is created, including any altar, elemental objects, or candles.

DELTA SIGMA THETA

The Pyramid Induction Ceremony (pg. 123)
Leader of the Minerva Circle: Now, the Sorors will encircle you. **As you stand in the center** of our strong circle of loving Sisterhood, you will join hands with each other, face the Sorors and listen as they sing the "Pyramid Hymn."[16]

Clothing during Rituals:

The previous and following statements are to highlight similarities and patterns. During rituals in Wicca and witchcraft, people are often required to wear robes. It is extremely common and expected. The purpose is to distinguish ritualistic and witchcraft activities from normal, everyday life. Rituals, in general, call for robe-wearing. In this organization, as an example, sorors are required to wear white and red robes. As stated in Preparation for the Initiation Ceremony (pg. 183), chapter officers wear white robes, Minerva Circle members wear red robes, sorors wear black attire, and candidates wear white attire.[16]

***

3. Secrets only belong to the Lord

Mysticism is a religious and spiritual concept in which people aim to experience the divine. People often use chants/mantras, meditation, and prayer to become united with the divine. Especially in the era of **Hellenism in ancient Greece**, rituals for ancient religions were kept secret (Merkur, 2024). Related to mysticism is esotericism, meaning esoteric doctrines or practices.[30] Esoteric doctrines and practices consist of secret knowledge amongst a small, select group of people. Esotericism is also related to mystic knowledge, various spiritualities, and the occult. I must include information about these concepts, because there is a prominent theme of secrecy and mysticism in the Divine 9 organizations, and Freemasonry (a foundation for a majority of fraternities and sororities that exist).

Many of the rituals describe "mysteries" of the organizations, secrets, and knowledge/wisdom/enlightenment— either belonging to the organization or the 'gods' associated with them. Also, in general, they have secret mottos, passwords, signs, grips, and handshakes.

An interesting scripture brought to mind when considering the hidden and secret things of the world was Mark 4:22 – "For there is nothing hidden which will not be revealed, nor has anything been kept secret but that it should come to light."

Definition of **mystical**

> ➢ relating to mystics or religious mysticism.
> - spiritually allegorical or symbolic; transcending human understanding.
> - relating to ancient religious mysteries or other occult or esoteric rites.
> - of hidden or esoteric meaning.[31]

Nothing about the Kingdom is secret. Does God have "secrets"? Of course; yet, He has given His children revelation through the Holy Spirit (1 Corinthians 2:9-10). He desires that we behold Him and draw close enough to know the depths of His heart and mind. As mentioned before, He is the light. We have been given His light, and scripture tells us that a city set on a hill cannot be hidden. A lamp is not lit to be put under a basket, but on a lampstand to give light to all in the house. Light must shine before men that God be GLORIFIED in the open (Matthew 5:16). The point is that God is not in the darkness. And when it comes to knowledge, secrets, and wisdom, He reigns as King over it all.

Ephesians 5:11-14 (CSB) –

Don't participate in the fruitless works of darkness, *but instead* ***expose them***. *For it is shameful even to mention what is* ***done by them in secret***. *Everything exposed by the light is made visible, for* ***what makes everything visible is light***.

Therefore it is said:

Get up, sleeper, *and rise up from the dead, and Christ will shine on you.*
(Most versions say: **Christ will give you light.**)

Luke 8:17 – *"For all that is secret will eventually be brought into the open, and everything that is concealed will be brought to light and made known to all."* (NLT)

Deuteronomy 29:29 – *"The secret things belong to the Lord our God…"*
> Secrets do not belong to any organization or false god.

Romans 11:33, 36 – *"Oh, how great are God's riches and wisdom and knowledge! How impossible it is for us to understand His decisions and His ways! For everything comes from Him and exists by His power and is intended for His glory. All glory to Him forever! Amen."* (NLT)

Proverbs 2:6 – *"For the LORD gives wisdom; from His mouth come knowledge and understanding…"*

Colossians 1:25-27 – *"…to fulfill the word of God, the <u>mystery which has been hidden from ages and from generations, but now has been revealed to His saints</u>. To them <u>God willed to make known</u> what are the riches of the glory of this mystery among the Gentiles: which is Christ in you…"*

ALPHA PHI ALPHA

Oath of Secrecy (pg. 6, 1976 pdf version)
I do solemnly swear (or aver) to keep absolutely secret the name and working of the Alpha Phi Alpha Fraternity, Incorporated.[14]

ALPHA KAPPA ALPHA

II. Obedience
Pilot: Candidates, are you willing to **enter deeper into the mysteries** of our organization? If so, state after me. "I am."[15]

(pg. 35)
Basileus: At this time our **deepest mysteries**, our **secret symbols**, will be revealed to you. Remember you have already vowed to keep them secret. The sorors who have been designated to explain the symbols now came forward.[15]

DELTA SIGMA THETA

Candidate: I, _____, do promise in the presence of <u>the Eternal Spirit of Truth</u>, and these finite witnesses, that I will never reveal in any manner whatsoever, for any purpose whatsoever, **any of the secrets**....[25]

ZETA PHI BETA

Ritual Ceremony II
Upon completion of the Course of Study, the chapter will present the neophytes with the official sorority pin, financial membership card, Handbook and Constitution, and membership Certificate and sorority's **secrets**.[17]

OMEGA PSI PHI

First Test (Discretion)
You… have written the mystic word…

Discretion, however, is but for the first step towards understanding **the mysteries of Omega**, so I must prepare you for the next unfoldments. Cling to me, I will be your guide. *Commandant leads the Neophyte out.*[19]

PHI BETA SIGMA

Initiation Ceremony
Chief Justice to the candidates: Cometh thou hither of thy own free will and accord to be initiated into **the mysteries and secrets** of this fraternity.[20]

VIII. FREEMASONRY, CONTINUED

HISTORY AND MORE INFORMATION

<u>Freemasonry, its teachings and beliefs, is not of God.</u>

A well-known book that explains the doctrines of Freemasonry is "Morals and Dogma of the Ancient and Accepted Scottish Rite of Freemasonry" written by Albert Pike. Albert Pike was a renowned lawyer and Confederate army general. He became a Mason in 1850, a Masonic **Grand High Priest** in 1853, was elected to the U.S. Supreme Council, **rewrote** many of the Masonic **rituals**, and studied the relationship between **spiritualism and Freemasonry** (Moneyhon, 2023). Pike is also the author of the book: "Hymns to the Gods: and Other Poems," focusing on the so-called divine nature of gods and goddesses, influenced by *Greek mythology*.

As of 2024, both books are available for free to the public domain. For "Morals and Dogma of the Ancient and Accepted Scottish Rite of Freemasonry," its overview on Google Books states that it "is a book of **esoteric philosophy** published by the Supreme Council, Thirty Third Degree, of the Scottish Rite, Southern Jurisdiction of the United States." Esotericism was previously discussed in the third part of Section VII.

Colossians 2:8 – "Beware lest anyone cheat you through **philosophy** and empty deceit, according to the **tradition of men**, according to the basic **principles of the world**, and **not ACCORDING to CHRIST**."

"This philosophy that threatened the Colossian Christians was a strange **eclectic** mix of early Gnosticism, **Greek philosophy**, local **mystery religions**, and **Jewish mysticism**. The philosophy threatening the Colossian Christians was so dangerous because it was not obviously sinful and licentious. It was high-sounding and seemed highly intelligent" (Guzik, n.d.).

If a doctrine is not according to and based on Christ, it is empty and should not be heeded.

It is so interesting that Guzik, in his commentary, decided to use the word eclectic. Eclectic describes anything, in general, that uses a mix of sources. In the philosophical sense, it describes philosophies that are based on diverse doctrines. That is exactly what the philosophies of Freemasonry are, eclectic, which further proves it is not of God.

➢ Masonic philosophies are connected to **Kabbalah (or Jewish) mysticism**.

- "There are profounder meanings concealed in the symbols of this Degree, connected with **the philosophical system of the Hebrew Kabalists**, which **you will learn** hereafter, if you should be so fortunate as to advance" (Pike, 1871, pg. 210-211).

➢ The Bible was said, in this text, to be **incomplete**; the **Kabbalah beliefs** are exalted.

- "**All truly dogmatic religions have issued from the Kabalah and return to it**; everything scientific and grand in the religious dreams of the Illuminati, Jacob Boehme, Swedenborg, Saint-Martin, and others, is **borrowed from the Kabalah; all the Masonic associations owe to it their Secrets and their Symbols**. The Kabalah alone consecrates the Alliance of the Universal Reason and the **Divine Word**... The Bible, with all the allegories it contains, expresses, in an **incomplete** and veiled manner only, the religious science of the Hebrews. The doctrine of Moses and the Prophets, identical at bottom with that of the ancient Egyptians, also had its outward meaning and its veils. The Hebrew books were written only to recall to memory the traditions; and they were written in Symbols unintelligible to the Profane... Thus was a second Bible born, unknown to, or rather uncomprehended by, the Christians; a collection, they say, of monstrous absurdities.... One is filled with admiration, on penetrating into the Sanctuary of the Kabalah, at seeing a doctrine so logical, so simple and at the same time so absolute" (Pike, 1871, pg. 744-745).

- "This is the **doctrine of the Kabalah**, with which you will no doubt **seek to make yourself acquainted**, as to the Creation. <u>The Absolute Deity, with the Kabalists, has no name</u> (Pike, 1871, pg. 744-745).

    - "...He Who is the Author of all, **has no name**" (Pike, 1871, pg. 749).

        - We know that this "Deity" being spoken of is not Yahweh. Our God cares about His name, and it is greatly exalted throughout all generations.

> Goodness is attributed to the Egyptian god Osiris.

- "'Everything good in nature comes from OSIRIS - order, harmony, and the favorable temperature of the seasons and celestial periods.' (page 476) Note: Osiris was the ancient

Egyptian god whose annual death and resurrection personified the self-renewing vitality and fertility of nature" (Capoccia, n.d.).

- Mark 10:18 – "Why do you call Me good? No one is good but One, that is, God."

- As seen in some of the D9 rituals as well, Freemasonry promotes syncretism and the embracing of beliefs of multiple gods. Furthermore, Freemasonry has *its own altars* and even *its own "God"* in which people of multiple faiths partake in and pray at.

  - "Masonry, around whose **altars** the Christian, the Hebrew, the Moslem, the Brahmin, the followers of Confucious and Zoroaster, **can assemble as brethren and unite in prayer to the one God** who is above all the Baalim, must needs leave it to each of its Initiates to look for the foundation of his faith and hope to the written scriptures of his own religion" (Pike, 1871, pg. 226).

    - As a believer, **people who worship other gods are not brethren**. The brethren are those in the Body of Christ, even as the Apostles addressed the Church as brethren in their epistles, because we are adopted as sons of God. Brothers, or brethren, share *the same blood*, coming from the same parent. We are brethren by the blood of Christ and adoption by our Father.

      - Hebrews 2:11 – "For both He who sanctifies and those who are being sanctified are all of one, for which reason He is not ashamed to **call them brethren**"
      - Romans 8:29 – "For whom He foreknew, He

also predestined to be conformed to the image of His Son, that He might be the firstborn among **many brethren**."
- John 1:12 – "But as many as received Him, to them He gave the right to become children of God, to those who believe in His name"
- Matthew 12:49-50 – "And He stretched out His hand toward His disciples and said, "Here are My mother and My brothers! For **whoever does the will of My Father in heaven is My brother...**"

- To "**unite** in prayer" with people who pray and communicate to other "gods" is to have fellowship with demons, according to 1 Corinthians 10:14-22. We know that our God is the only true and living God; what others are believing they are praying to as "God(s)" are just the spirits behind the altars erected to those believed deities. Also, this contradicts God's instructions to come out from among them, to be consecrated and separate, and to not be unequally yoked or UNITED. Two cannot walk together unless they agree. So, if you unite in prayer and the partaking of altars with people who are not true brethren, you are agreeing with the spirits behind their gods. Christ and the 'god' of this world (Satan) have no agreement. We must instead flee from any forms of idolatry. This is speaking of *spiritual fellowship*.

  - 1 Corinthians 10:14-22 – "Therefore, my beloved, **flee from idolatry**. I speak as to wise men; judge for yourselves what I say. The cup of blessing which we bless, is it not the communion of the blood of Christ? The bread which we break, is it not the communion of the body of Christ? For we, though many, are one bread and one body; for we all partake of that one bread. Observe Israel after the flesh: are not those who eat of the sacrifices **partakers of the altar?** What am I saying then? That an idol is anything, or what is offered to idols is anything? Rather, that the things which the **GENTILES** *(i.e. the 'Moslem,' Brahmin, etc.)* **SACRIFICE THEY SACRIFICE TO DEMONS and NOT TO GOD**, and I do not want you to have **FELLOWSHIP WITH DEMONS**. <u>You cannot drink the cup of the Lord and the cup of demons; you cannot partake of the Lord's table and of the table of demons.</u> Or do we **PROVOKE THE LORD TO JEALOUSY?** Are we stronger than He?"

- 2 Corinthians 6:14-18 – ***Do not be unequally yoked together with unbelievers***. *For what **fellowship** has **righteousness with lawlessness**? And what **communion** has **light with darkness**? And what accord has Christ with Belial? Or what part has a **believer with an unbeliever**? And what **agreement** has the **temple of God with idols**? For you are the temple of the living God. As God has said: "I will dwell in them and walk among them. I will be their God, and they shall be My people." Therefore **"Come out from among them and be separate, says the Lord. Do not touch what is unclean, and I will receive you."**

- "The word, Baalim, is simply defined as 'false god or idol'. The Masonic author has included the God of the Christian in that category" (Capoccia, n.d.). Therefore, this text is saying that the God of the Christian is false and inferior to the Mason's god.

➢ The Masonic god is not the same God the Believer follows, Yahweh, Who is One with Jesus Christ. This philosophical book on Masonic morals mentions the gods of multiple faiths together (including a mention of Jesus Christ) and says that each faith acknowledges their own truth; but with Masonry, there is instead its own god and its own doctrine. Jesus Christ is explicitly separated from their acknowledgment of who "God" is. One way to know if *the spirit* behind something is of God is to test the spirit and to see if the source confesses Jesus Christ's coming in the flesh.

1 John 4:1-3, 6 – "Beloved, do not believe every spirit, but test the spirits, **whether they are of God**; because many false prophets have gone out into the world. By this you know the Spirit of God: <u>Every spirit that **confesses** that Jesus Christ has come in the flesh is of God, and every spirit that **does not confess** that Jesus Christ has come in the flesh is not of God.</u> And this is the *spirit* of the Antichrist, which you have heard was coming, and is now already in the world... [By this] we know the spirit of truth and the spirit of error."

- "While the Indian tells us that Parabrahma, Brahm, and Paratma were the first Triune God...
  ...the Buddhists of the God Sakya, a Trinity composed of Buddha, Dharma, and Sanga...
  ...the Ancient Prussian points to *his* Triune God, *Perkoun, Pikollos, and Potrimpos*...
  And while <u>the pious Christian believes</u> that the Word dwelt in the Mortal Body of Jesus of Nazareth...

While **all these** faiths assert **their** claims to the exclusive possession of the Truth, **Masonry inculcates its old doctrine, and no more**... that God is One..." (Pike, 1871, pg. 576)

- ➢ These doctrines exalt human consciousness and instinct as a spiritual foundation, but not Jesus and (/who is) the Word of God. This completely contradicts God's truths.

    - "The Mason does not pretend to dogmatic certainty..." (Pike, 1871, pg. 226)

        - As followers of Christ, we are certain in the Word and truths of God.

    - "He [the Mason] considers that if there were **no written revelation**, he could safely rest the hopes that animate him and the principles that guide him, on the deductions of reason and the convictions of instinct and consciousness. He can find a **sure foundation** for his religious belief, **in these deductions of reason and the convictions of the heart**. For reason proves to him the existence and attributes of God; and those spiritual instincts which he feels are **the voice of God** in his soul infuse into his mind a sense of his relation to God..." (Pike, 1871, pg. 226)

        - As followers of Christ, there is no need to consider there being no written revelation. Also, the *voice of God* is found in His word, not our *own* feelings and reasonings.

            - 2 Timothy 3:13-17 – "But evil men and impostors will grow worse and worse,

deceiving and being deceived. But you must continue** in the things which you have learned and **been assured of**, knowing from whom you have learned them, and that from childhood you have known **the Holy Scriptures**, which are able to make you wise for salvation through faith which is in Christ Jesus. **All Scripture is given by inspiration of God**, and is **profitable for <u>doctrine</u>**, for reproof, for correction, for instruction in righteousness, that the man of God may be complete, thoroughly equipped for every good work."
  - Mark 13:31 – "Heaven and earth will pass away, but My words will by no means pass away."
  - Psalms 119:105 – "Your word is a lamp to my feet and a light to my path."

- Jesus Christ is the only foundation for our religious belief.

  - 1 Corinthians 3:11 – **"For no other foundation can anyone lay than that which is laid, which is Jesus Christ."**

- We cannot trust in our *own* convictions of our *own* consciousness and our *own* hearts.

  - Jeremiah 17:9 – **"The heart is *deceitful above all things*, and *desperately wicked*; who can know it?"**

- ➤ Keeping these doctrines and dogmas in mind, note that Freemasonry has temples of religion.

  - "Every Masonic Temple is a Temple of Religion; and its teachings are instructions in religion... Here we meet as brethren..." (Pike, 1871, pg. 213)

<u>Most Greek-lettered fraternities and sororities in America (both Panhellenic Council and NPHC) were modeled upon Freemasonry.</u>

The first collegiate fraternity founded in America was Phi Beta Kappa in 1776 at the College of William and Mary in Williamsburg, VA. There are many connections that show the association between American Greek-lettered organizations and Freemasonry.

A Scottish Rite of Freemasonry Intern wrote about Phi Beta Kappa in the Scottish Rite journal saying:

> This group eventually would be named the Phi Beta Kappa Society, a fraternity that many credit with the tradition of naming American college societies after initials of 'secret' Greek mottos, hence 'Greek-letter fraternities.' **What many do not know, however, is that Phi Beta Kappa's origin had a strong Masonic influence.** While the principal founder John Heath himself was not a Mason (as he was only 15 at the time), another co-founder, Thomas Smith was a Mason. Smith belonged to Williamsburg Masonic Lodge before he joined Heath as a founding member of Phi Beta Kappa. Within the next year, nine of the founding members would be raised as Master Masons, and over a dozen of the subsequent 50 members would be associated with both organizations in the years to come. Today, Phi Beta Kappa has 284 active chapters across the United States. **Since its founding, over 150 similar organizations would emerge on college campuses across the country, with several of them being established by Brother Mason.** (Gentil, 2016, pg. 8-9)

As a side note, this journal entry by the intern was exploring undergraduate fraternities and sororities founded by Masons or having significant Masonic influence. It's all about the roots. Many D9 organizations are mentioned in this writing such as:

Alpha Phi Alpha (the **first** D9 organization) –

> "In December 1905, principal founder Charles Poindexter met with 15 students, which included Vertner Tandy, a Prince Hall Mason from Lexington, Kentucky, and George B. Kelley who was **also active in Masonic circles** and also an employee of Beta Theta Pi, in order to form an organization that developed leaders and promoted brotherhood… In fact, **the organization held its first initiation in a Masonic lodge** in Ithaca, New York. The legend has it that while in the Masonic lodge, they opened up the lockers and **used the various Masonic regalia** that was found inside in order to **enhance their own ritual**…" (Gentil, 2016, p. 10)

Phi Beta Sigma –

> "**(Founder A. Langston Taylor was an active Mason**, but it is not known whether or not he was a Mason during his undergraduate career.) **The organization states that its 'Practices are based upon Masonic influence.'**" (Gentil, 2016, pg. 11)

>> According to the Beta Alpha chapter of Phi Beta Sigma's website, "…Masonic influences can still be seen in the step process as well as the pledge process of most Black Greek Lettered Organizations" (Beta Alpha Chapter, n.d.).

Omega Psi Phi –

> "**The principal founder of this fraternity was Edgar Amos Love, a Prince Hall Freemason** who was also a

founding member of Corinthian Lodge No. 68 in Washington, DC." (Gentil, 2016, pg. 11)

Later in this section includes an explanation on how Freemasonry was even introduced to the African American community and what Prince Hall Freemasonry is.

In general, what the Masonic order modeled for the fraternities and sororities to come was a focus on the "light" (enlightenment/higher knowledge), secrecy, oaths and rituals for initiates, and the formation of additional chapters of a same organization (Stafford, 2007). The Phi Beta Kappa letters stand for Philosophia Biou Kybernetes which means, "Love of Wisdom, the Guide of Life," as many organizations have mottos regarding wisdom, guidance, life, and again, light. These are not attributed to Jesus Christ but more so to the "Supreme Being," expressed in both Masonic and Phi Beta Kappa rituals (Stafford, 2007). Note that two of the fraternity's founders were part of Freemasonry.

In regards to additional chapters, more were established at Yale, Harvard, and Dartmouth in 1780, 1781, and 1787 respectively.

Also established at Yale University was the **Skull and Bones secret society** (also known as the **Brotherhood of Death**) in 1832 by co-founders William Russell and Alphanso Taft. It was originally named the Eulogian Club, as the secret society gave homage to **Eulogia** (known as the **goddess** of eloquence). The monument of the society is the "Tomb." Written on part of the tomb is instructions to "Pass through the sacred pillars of **Hercules** and approach the **Temple**. Take the right Book in your left hand… (Richards, 2015)." Notice the incorporation of Greco-Roman deities and connotations of sacredness, i.e., temple. Moreover, association with pagan deities in the current fraternal organizations and secret societies is nothing new.

There are two main descriptions of the initial founding of the secret society. Some accounts say that there was a dispute related to the Phi Beta Kappa chapter at Yale. Other accounts recall that Russell studied abroad in Germany where he was inspired by German and other European secret societies. These societies and clubs were "mystical and elite" (Stephey, M.J.).

The fraternal order is represented by an image of a skull and crossbones, including the number 322 (which simply is known to refer to the death of Demosthenes, Greek orator, in 322 B.C.). Across cultures in general, the skull and crossbones symbol represents death. Sometimes, it represents poison or a hazard warning for something deadly.

Note. From Yale University Archives 中文：來源：耶魯大學檔案館, Public domain, via Wikimedia Commons

The 'skull and crossbones' is known to be a symbol of Masonic application and association, "For it both conceals and reveals genuine mysteries pertaining to our Craft" (Newman, 2014).

We see this skull and crossbones symbol represented in many more secret societies through their crests and coat of arms. Feel free to do a Google search to see the symbols visually. Examples are Phi Kappa Sigma, Chi Omega, and ***Sigma Gamma Rho***.

How was Freemasonry introduced to the African American community?

Prince Hall was a former (turned freed) slave, Black leader, and abolitionist during The American Revolution/Revolutionary War (1770s). "Prince Hall was attracted to the values and opportunities of Freemasonry and sought to join the city's Masonic lodges. He was denied membership but did not let this obstacle prevent him from pursuing the fraternity's rich lessons. Not to be deterred, Hall, along with fourteen other African Americans who had also been rejected by the lodges of Boston lodges, approached a Masonic lodge affiliated with British soldiers who occupied the city at that time. This British lodge accepted and initiated them that same year, and they remained active members until the Revolutionary War ended" (Scottish Rite Freemasonry, NMJ, n.d.). Hall founded the first lodge of black Freemasonry, eventually called Prince Hall Freemasonry. These Freemasons practice "the secret rituals and moral teachings" of the original Freemasonry (NMAAHC, n.d.).

Quotes from the paper by Merchang and Rich (2001):

- ➤ www.geocities.com described in "Why Pledge a Fraternity?" (as citied in Merchang & Rich, 2001) that "One organization in particular that was working to improve the condition of life for those individuals was an order known as Free and Accepted Masons. While striving towards the upliftment of the quality of life for Blacks, this organization was somewhat limited in what it could do because of the requirements for membership. Only males who had reached the age of 21 and had proven themselves to be of good character were allowed to apply for membership, which meant that mostly blue collar workers could be Masons.

However, our founders (ALL organizations) had visions as to how to create a shortcut, or place a stepping stone if you would, for the Masonic fraternity."

- A history of Phi Beta Sigma claims that stepping "began with singing or chanting associated with the process of crossing the burning sands," and the phrase "burning sands" which is widespread in African American fraternities has been associated with Masonic Shrine initiations since the late nineteenth century (Wilson, 1996; cited in Merchang & Rich, 2001). The African American Shriners had a great influence on black culture, particularly on Moorish Science and hence indirectly on the Nation of Islam.

According to A.E.A.O.N.M.S.,

- John G Jones was a thirty-three degreed Mason, the highest colored mason in America. He founded African American Shriners which is also called the Ancient Egyptian Arabic Order, the Nobles Mystic Shrine. This is related to mysticism.
- "John George Jones, the founder, is said to have been introduced to the ritualistic mysteries of the Order by one Ali Rofelt Pasha, Deputy, and a representative from the Grand Council of Arabia, during the World's Colombian Exposition in Chicago in 1893. Within days of this honor, Noble Jones, along with 13 other Prince Hall Masons, would organize Palestine Temple in the Apollo Hall on State Street, which would lead to the establishment

of the Imperial Grand Council of Prince Hall Shriners, Ancient Arabic Order Nobles Mystic Shrine (A.A.O.N.M.S.) on June 10, 1893. Over the next several months, Noble John G. Jones would spend time traveling and setting up Prince Hall Shrine Temples in cities across the United States" (A.E.A.O.N.M.S., n.d.).

"Shrines" and "shriners" are mentioned significantly throughout this book. It is important to note that a shrine is a place of worship, often built for pagan gods. Shriners gather at Shrine clubs and places called Shrine. It is important to investigate this.

The black Boulé (Sigma Pi Phi), a Black Greek-Lettered Organization, immediately preceded the founding and inspiration of the Divine 9 collegiate organizations. It was founded in 1904, two years before Alpha Phi Alpha. The principal founder was Henry McKee Minton who patterned the fraternity off of Skull and Bones, which of course has many similarities to Freemasonry. Charles H. Wesley was a member of the Boulé, Alpha Phi Alpha, Prince Hall Freemasonry, and other fraternal organizations. He was a historian who wrote many books on African-American history, including "History of Sigma Pi Phi: First of the Negro-American Greek-letter Fraternities" and "The History of Alpha Phi Alpha." On page 28 of his historical account of the Boulé, Wesley quotes Minton's purpose of creating the organization, where Minton stated that he wanted to create an organization which would partake of "the tenets of Skull and Bones at Yale and Phi Beta Kappa." Note that a tenet is "a principle, belief, or doctrine generally held to be true, especially one held in common by members of an organization, movement, or profession."[32] Further on page 38, Wesley states that "reliance was placed upon Greek history and tradition" in the building of the organization (Wesley, 1969, as cited in The Boule, n.d.). From the Boulé founders placing reliance on Greek tradition to Alpha Phi Alpha founders incorporating Masonic elements in their rituals, pagan/European culture and Freemasonry are a significant foundation to D9 and other Greek-lettered organizations today. D9 members often say that the only Greek thing about the organizations is the letters, but we see it is much deeper than that.

Moreover, the NPHC organizations were intentionally modeled upon both Freemasonry and ancient Greek practices/traditions. Both in the past and today, these organizations promote membership in Masonic orders.

Quotes:

> "The most **direct line of descent** from Greek societies to America is **the Freemasons** (called Masons). Historians of American fraternities and sororities trace **most of our rituals, ceremonies and rites to the Masons.** An examination of Masonic rituals open to scholars suggest(s) that **our Founders** were also **influenced** by **Masonic ritual, symbolism** and **initiation** experiences."
>
> – (Delta Sigma Theta Sorority, INC., GRAND CHAPTER, CANDIDATE SYLLABUS, 1990, pg. 30)

> "**Our founders** were well aware of the need to **transfuse the ideals** of **Greek moral virtues** with the later concepts of brotherhood and love. That is why they clearly wrote: 'We are a sisterhood founded on Christian principles...'"
>
> – (Delta Sigma Theta Sorority, INC., GRAND CHAPTER, CANDIDATE SYLLABUS, 1990, pg. 30)

"**Black Greek-Lettered Organizations (BGLO) are a byproduct of Freemasonry**, and the rituals are derived from it. The symbol they have chosen to represent their god is the "All Seeing Eye," which the Egyptians used to represent the pagan god, Osiris. Now Masons/Eastern Stars will claim to be Christian, just like BGLOs do, and will use The Bible in their ceremonies and rituals. However, it is the mixing of holy with the profane, since all these actually worship the "spirit" of their organization. Moreover, they also accept whatever belief a person has (sometimes even changing the rituals to fit), which is clearly not TRUE Christianity" (OFATM, n.d.).

> Resource for information on Freemasonry conflicting with Christianity: http://www.ephesians5-11.org/

Iota Phi Theta:

> This organization's founder(s) are still alive today. There is an article on Lonnie C. Spruill Jr. recently becoming a master mason (Watch the Yard, 2024). This indicates that he was already a (lower-degree) Mason. There is a theme between the founders of these organizations being a part of Freemasonry, Order of the Eastern Stars, and founding the Greek Letter organizations.

Black women members of Order of the Eastern Star:

"The Order of the Eastern Star was established in Boston in 1850 as an auxiliary organization for wives, mothers, daughters, and sisters of Freemasons. It became affiliated with the Prince Hall Masons in 1874 through the founding of the Queen Esther Chapter No. 1 in Washington, D.C. The Eastern Star conducts its own philanthropic and community service activities, as well as supporting the work of the male lodges" (NMAAHC, n.d.). The founders of many of the D9 organizations were members of Prince Hall Freemasonry and Order of the Eastern Star. There is a clear link between the rituals, ideals, and practices of these father/mother organizations and the BGLOs.

***

<u>Freemasonry's rites and rituals have too much mixture with the pagan world.</u>

"Like other secret societies, Freemasonry is known for its elaborate system of codes, symbols, and rituals. For African American members, Masonic teachings that drew on the Bible reinforced the Christian values preached in the Black churches. Other Masonic traditions that celebrated the **knowledge of ancient civilizations, including Egypt**, offering a prideful **connection to African cultural heritage**…"

– Quote from the National Museum of African American History (NMAAHC, n.d.)

Do you see the pattern here? Like the rituals and symbolisms in various BGLOs, there is a celebration of knowledge of ancient civilizations such as Egypt.

"You must not do as they do in Egypt, where you used to live, and you must not do as they do in the land of Canaan, where I am bringing you. Do not follow their practices. You must obey my laws and be careful to follow my decrees. I am the Lord your God." – Leviticus 18:3-4 NIV

Freemasonry refers to God as the GAOTU (Grand Architect of the Universe) and people from all religions join the organization. There are 'Christian' Lodges, Muslim Lodges, and Lodges of all the other religions who have Masonic accreditation. This is syncretism, which was mentioned previously and is seen in the fraternities and sororities.

Example of a Ritual/Rite: Hot Sands Ceremony (Freemasonry) and Crossing the Burning Sands (D9):

One of the initiation rituals in becoming a Shriner (including Prince Hall Shriners) in Freemasonry is to cross over "Hot Sands." It has been said that this ritual uses electricity and is a hazing rite, having been banned in various lodges since about 2012. Other sources say it has ceased due to controversy surrounding lawsuits and even references in the ritual to the Islamic religion (Lahners, 2021). Crossing the burning sands is respective to the D9. Part of its meaning is that an initiate has officially "crossed over" into membership of the organization. For many chapters, this has included a physical ritual of "crossing the burning sands" and is known to allude to traveling by foot across Egypt or other African territories. This is not a total explanation of this concept, as rituals have their secret meanings. Note, again, that author Merchang stated in 2001, "The phrase 'burning sands' which is widespread in African American fraternities has been associated with Masonic Shrine initiations since the late nineteenth century."

"**Secret societies** have six common elements. (1) **SECRECY**, particularly as to forms and ceremonies. (2) EXCLUSIVENESS, with strict admission requirements. (3)HIERARCHICAL, requiring a progressive status system. (4) ORDEAL, calling for an **Initiation** trial of greater or less rigorousness. (5) **MYTHIC ORIGIN**, sometimes semi-factual, sometimes outright imaginary. (6) SELF-CONTAINED, by separating themselves from the common world." – Quoted from (Merchang & Rich 2001) who quoted "Secrecy," Royal Arch Mason, Vol. 18 No.4, Winter 1994, 118.

IX. COMMON QUESTIONS, STATEMENTS, AND REBUTTALS

1. *"You take oaths in professional fields: medicine (Hippocratic Oath); legal system (legal oaths), military, etc."*

There are various types of oaths taken today, especially in court and professional fields. An oath is a solemn and sacred promise. It is true in the New Testament that Jesus taught about and forbade oaths because of the gravity of oaths.

> Matthew 5:33-36 – "Again you have heard that it was said to those of old, 'You shall not swear falsely, but shall perform your oaths to the Lord.' But I say to you, do not swear at all: neither by heaven, for it is God's throne; nor by the earth, for it is His footstool; nor by Jerusalem, for it is the city of the great King. Nor shall you swear by your head…"

A professional or career-centered oath is much different than a ritualistic oath which is often spoken before an altar, in a secret society. This is because the former has a carnal purpose, the latter is spiritual. Secondly, there is legally an option in the United States to take an Affirmation in place of an oath, especially for religious reasons. Note that an oath is "often invoking a **divine witness**" according to the Oxford definition; more specifically, it is "a solemn or formal declaration **invoking God (or a god, or other object of reverence)** as witness to the truth of a statement, or to **the <u>binding</u> nature** of a promise or undertaking."[33] This is why the scriptures mention not swearing by **"heavenly"** things, deities especially.

***

2. *"How can a Christian be cursed or afflicted by spiritual covenants when we are under the covenant of the blood of Jesus Christ?"*

    According to Galatians 3:10-14, we are redeemed from the curse of the law. This is referring to the Mosaic Law which was given on tablets to the nation of Israel with instruction on how to engage God through sacrifices and ceremonies. Our redemption through Jesus's blood is what gives us access to worship and know God through His Son. Jesus is now the sacrifice, no longer goats and rams. In what mankind could not perfectly live up to, including priestly duties, Jesus was and is perfect. He was and is the fulfillment.

    It is no longer our works that make us righteous. Our belief and faith in Jesus, the gift of salvation, and the sanctification of the Holy Spirit produce a result and fruit of good works. Jesus saves us; we don't save ourselves. As we abide in Him, we are made holy and acceptable to God. We are yielded to His Spirit and follow His ways. Moreover, we worship God and live in righteousness through faith in Him.

    Let me emphasize that the "Law" is not bad. It just no longer curses us because of redemption. And because of the New Covenant, there is a new context in which we observe laws. For example, there is still sacrifice, but Jesus Himself is the sacrifice in which we are atoned for sins. Furthermore, we understand the differences between moral, ceremonial, and sacrificial laws. The Israelites observed many ordinances to consecrate and separate themselves as holy from the heathen nations. Now, we worship God and separate ourselves unto Him by presenting our bodies as a living sacrifice. We consecrate ourselves by allowing our minds to be renewed and transformed according to the Word of God (yes, His commands!), coming out from among the world and the world's ways. The circumcision of the Holy Spirit has allowed us to have God's laws written on our hearts and no longer tablets of stone (again, the giving of Mosaic Law). We worship Him now in SPIRIT. We communicate with Him through the SPIRIT. We thank God for access and intimacy with Him!

Regarding curses, covenants, demons, etc., the spiritual realm operates based on legal rights. The Bible says that the wages of sin is death. Sin has consequences that do not lead to life, but death (not always physical death but things like bondage, affliction, lack of peace, etc.). The enemy roams around like a roaring lion, seeking whom he may devour, whom he may [kill, and] destroy. We will come back to this point. The enemy often gains access to people when a door is opened through sin. Furthermore, when *you open* the door to the enemy, he is *allowed* to come in.

This is one of the reasons why God spoke through Paul in 2 Corinthians 6, admonishing the Corinthians to be holy, to touch no unclean thing, and to 'come out from among them.' It is a reason why we receive a reminder that our bodies are temples and houses of God. What we engage our temples (minds, bodies) with matters. This call to holiness is both for 1) God and 2) our protection.

1. The Holy Spirit, who resides in us, is grieved when its place of residence (our bodies) mixes itself with unclean, unholy things.
2. Spirits, demonic spirits, always look for a place to dwell, a place to be hosted. They seek to inhabit man, man's minds and flesh. Matthew 12:43-44 says, "When an unclean spirit goes out of a man, he goes through dry places, seeking rest, and finds none. Then he says, 'I will return to my house from which I came.'" It is definitely possible, common even, for demons to make

their dwelling places in Christians because there is a distinction between Spirit and flesh. Why else would Paul discuss the war between Spirit and flesh (Galatians 5) and how we must live and walk in the Spirit? Why else are we told that we must renew our minds to be transformed (Romans 12)? Why else does sanctification occur in multiple dimensions: spirit, soul, and body? "Now may the God of peace Himself sanctify you completely; and may your whole spirit, soul, and body be preserved blameless at the coming of our Lord Jesus Christ," 1 Thessalonians 5:23. Why else would the Apostle Peter warn Christians to be sober and vigilant, to keep careful watch of our adversary the devil roaming about to see whom he may devour? He is looking to devour the people of God! If our minds are not sober and we don't resist him, he will not flee. He will stay when there is a door and access.

> 1 Peter 5:8-9 – *"Be sober, be vigilant; because YOUR adversary the devil walks around like a roaring lion, seeking whom he may devour. Resist him, steadfast in the faith…"*

> James 4:7 – *"Therefore submit to God. Resist the devil and he will flee from you."*

For practical examples, when you engage in porn and masturbation, spirits of lust are welcomed to your mind and body. When you fail to forgive others, your heart may be plagued by bitterness and resentment. When you make sacrifices in other spiritualities or new age practices, evil spirits are welcomed to torment you. When you perform a witchcraft spell, witchcraft spirits will come. Regarding these organizations and rituals, whatever spirits are associated with them come to make their home. In these rituals, chants, paraphernalia, and all the like, **the enemy is not resisted but welcomed**. He deceives people into not only welcoming him but vowing their will and submission to his kingdom. Whatever is not rooted in God is rooted in the kingdom of darkness. It's hard to submit to God in an area where you have already vowed and bowed/kneeled your submission to the world.

Lastly, the sin of idolatry alone still leads to the 'death' previously mentioned, simply because it is a sin. All the chants, gods on the crests, and idolatrous practices mentioned in this book violate the command that proclaims we should not have any other gods before, besides, or alongside the One true God.

***

3. *"There is no evidence of curses or bondage in my life…"* | A thought on Bloodlines and Legacy:

I implore you to evaluate the physical, spiritual, mental, emotional, and relational aspects of your life. Do you or does anything in your life lack peace? Are there any strongholds or struggles such as with mental health (anxiety, depression)? If you are a parent or want to become one, have you or has your partner had healthy pregnancies and births? Do you deal with any sins such as lust? If you do deal with anything mentioned above or similar, no, it is not always traced back to involvement in a Greek Lettered Organization. By no means am I mentioning these things to generalize or desensitize the real-life difficulties that people encounter, whether a member or not. It is just good to consider and evaluate, in case a root to a difficulty you've dealt with possibly went unchecked, such as via joining a GLO. This does not apply to everyone.

Maybe life has been great and you have not dealt with any issues that stemmed from the covenants made in your organization. The issue remaining is with your bloodline. Not only did God reveal through the dream He gave me, but through His word that sin affects bloodlines. Another spiritual law to observe is the way sin travels through generations.

Looking back to the commandments about idolatry, we see Exodus 20:3-6 – "You shall have no other gods before Me. You shall not make for yourself a carved image - any likeness of anything that is in heaven above, or that is in the earth beneath, or that is in the water under the earth; **you shall not bow down** to them nor serve them. For I, the Lord your God, am a jealous God, **visiting the iniquity of the fathers upon the children to the third and fourth generations** of those who hate Me, but showing mercy to thousands, to those who love Me and keep My commandments." Numbers 14:18 says, "The Lord is longsuffering and abundant in mercy, forgiving iniquity and transgression; but He by no means clears the guilty, visiting the iniquity of the fathers on the children to the third and fourth generation."

Let's unpack these scriptures just a bit more. For context, the nation of Israel was commanded not to bow down to or serve other gods, even likeness of 'gods' or physical images of them. Those are examples of iniquity and transgression. To commit these acts was to hate Him. On the contrary, to love Him is to obey His commandments.

I don't mention these scriptures to say that God is holding all children of idolatrous fathers personally accountable and guilty for their ancestors' sins. When a descendant chooses righteousness, God shows mercy. That is why in Numbers, it says the iniquity and transgression is forgiven. Also, refer to Ezekiel 18:19-32 where it explains that the son does not have to bear the guilt of his father if he does what is just. God desires that all may live and receive His abundant mercy!

Moreover, the reason I am mentioning these scriptures about iniquity and generations is because they hint to the spiritual principle of sin traveling generationally. Sin affects children and bloodlines. Patterns and cycles are seen to be replicated in descendants, even biologically. You find people being careful not to indulge in alcohol if they have a history of addiction and alcoholism in the family. If someone's parent and grandparent dealt with things such as anger or jealousy, for example, we sometimes see that person also dealing with anger or jealousy. In the Bible, Abraham's bloodline had a pattern of lying. Abraham lied about his wife, Sarah, being his sister. His son Isaac lied about his wife, Rebekah, being his sister.

In other words, patterns of sin can cause a bloodline to be susceptible to patterns of sin. If the ancestor/father does not repent for his iniquity, it is more likely that their children will be affected by that iniquity, whether that be the susceptibility to commit the same sins or through demons looking for a new man to afflict. Patterns repeat themselves, but repentance breaks the pattern. The covering of the blood of Jesus is sufficient. It is sufficient for physical and spiritual healing, for access to the Father, for eternal life, and so much more. It also gives us the power to break patterns and strongholds that were brought about by free will and open doors. The devil, your adversary and accuser, looks for ways to attack you through places that were not submitted to God because that is where he can gain access.

No wonder the Divine 9 culture pushes so hard for "legacy," and making sure your children, and your children's children, join the same organizations. If the enemy can't afflict you, he at least wants to afflict the descendants in your bloodline. The Kingdom of God spreads and continues through bloodlines. God desires godly offspring and that His people are fruitful and multiply. If the enemy can attack the children of God, he can attempt to hinder the fruitfulness of our Kingdom.

But, God's power is so redemptive. The Bible says in Proverbs 11:9 that through knowledge, the just (or righteous) shall be delivered. One of the reasons that the Holy Spirit leads us into all truth is so that we can have life and have it more abundantly. This is what Jesus came for. The truth sets us free, especially free from bondage. Lastly, the blood of Jesus is a continual force in our lives, as we stay in fellowship with the Father, working out our own salvation. I would like to highlight a passage the Apostle John wrote about walking in fellowship with God and this continual cleansing from the blood of Jesus.

1 John 1:4-9 – "And these things we write to you **that your joy**

may be full. This is the message which we have heard from Him and declare to you, that God is light and in Him is no darkness at all. If we say that we have fellowship with Him, and walk in darkness, we lie and do not practice the truth. But if we walk in the light as He is in the light, we have fellowship with one another, and **the blood of Jesus Christ, His Son, cleanses us from all sin.** If we say that we have no sin, we deceive ourselves, and the truth is not in us. If we confess our sins, **He is faithful and just to forgive us our sins and to cleanse us from all unrighteousness.**" Praise God!

***

4. *"But, my Pastor is Greek."*

Many people express that membership in fraternities and sororities is acceptable for Christians because leaders in the Body of Christ are members. It is true that many leaders, such as pastors, are still involved. I do not agree with spiritual leaders being members of GLOs and the D9. That is because I believe that no Christian should be a member. With leaders, this is even more so, because Christians look up to leaders as an example.

We must note that leaders are not perfect, no Christian is. Until more recent years, the truths about Greek life were not as heavily discussed in general or in the Church. That is one of the advantages (to Satan's kingdom) of it being so 'secretive.' The secrecy made it difficult and less common to expose the darkness to the light. Deception is not beyond someone just because they are a leader. Idolatry is not beyond someone just because they are a leader. This is why we must continually check our hearts.

And speaking of legacy, you will often find that the leaders and pastors who are Greek have parents and grandparents that were

Greek before them. The D9 is a staple in Black culture. It is so historical and has been accepted in the Church for decades. For so long, it has been easy to miss the subtle areas of darkness and deception.

Exodus 32 gives us a biblical example of a leader falling short. Aaron, Moses's brother, was appointed as a high priest among the Israelites. When Moses was away from the Israelites and took a long time (40 days) to come down from the mountain, Aaron received much pressure from the people. They were anxious for an answer, so anxious that they sought gods (vs.1) to lead them to the Promised Land. They lost their faith in God and were depending on what they could physically see. Aaron made the golden calf from gold jewelry and the Israelites worshiped it. Aaron shows us that it is possible to be a leader, a spokesperson for God, and anointed, but to still fall short.

Pray for the leaders in the Body of Christ, and not just the ones who are Greek either. Teaching and guiding a flock is not a light task.

Most importantly, <u>Jesus is the standard</u>, not man. We follow our leaders as they follow Christ, as they follow what Jesus has commanded.

***

5. *Many groups (or chapters and lines) within the organizations have gone to church together, prayed and hosted Christian events together. People also recount seeing people come to Christ during or after their initiation process. A common question I hear is, "What if God wanted to use me or send me in the organization to be a light in the dark places and change the things that are not of God?"*

Going to church/Christian events and praying is a good gesture, but it does not necessarily mean that God is pleased. God spoke in the Bible of people that honor Him with their lips, but their hearts are far from Him. Secondly, God delights more in obedience than sacrifice (1 Samuel 15:22). Doing "Christian things" such as attending a church service is simply vain worship if one's heart is far from God and they are actively disobeying Him. Jesus said to love Him is to keep His commandments. There is a type of worship and sacrifice that God desires— having a contrite heart. To be contrite is to be repentant, humble, and express remorse. It is to be broken. It is to be willing to give up anything that God says He is displeased with because *your heart wants Him more than anything*.

It is definitely possible for people to encounter Christ during a Greek organization membership process. It is usually a challenging experience, and people find themselves calling on God for strength and guidance. Or, people simply meet other Christians through connections made in Greek life. God can meet someone anywhere. He's encountered people in the streets, at clubs, and all kinds of places. It does not mean it was His will for them to be in those places, partaking of those things. But once they have come to Christ, scripture says, "we know that all things work together for good to those who love God, to those who are [the] called according to His purpose (Romans 8:28)."

<u>God is powerful enough to save people in a pure way.</u> He doesn't need His people to sin in order to save or influence others that are in sin. It is AMAZING when a soul is saved! But, what about their journey after they accept Christ? With the advocacy for membership in Greek organizations on the basis of salvations, new believers that are Greek may feel comfortable staying in sin after they accept the gift of salvation. It is like they are enabled to stay Greek — even though God is not pleased with it and they've opened the door to the kingdom of darkness — because their salvation occurred while they were Greek.

It is like saying it is okay to do sinful clubbing activities to reach and evangelize to club-goers who are doing the respective sinful activities. I've seen people evangelize outside nightclubs, and I find nothing wrong with that. The issue is when you actually fellowship and partake of the same things as the people who are sinning. Unfortunately, with Greek life, to be amongst people during their process, you must be a part of the process as well. Did you know that salt, in its purest, natural form, cannot lose its flavor unless it has additives, or unless something like water dissolved or diluted it? Matthew 5:13 says, "You are the salt of the earth; but if the salt loses its flavor, how shall it be seasoned? It is then good for nothing but to be thrown out and trampled underfoot by men." This chapter continues to talk about believers being the light of the world. Be salt and light. People will see Jesus in you without you having to do what they do.

***

6. *"We sang songs and said different things, but I didn't actually mean it…"*

Jesus said in Matthew 12:36, "But I say to you that for every idle word men may speak, they will give account of it in the day of judgment." Every word counts, especially words spoken in pledges, oaths, and vows. Secondly, death and life are in the power of the tongue. Whether your speech is life-giving and godly or idle and careless, fruit will be yielded (Proverbs 18:21).

We are saved by the confession of our mouths that Jesus is Lord. As the enemy tries to copy the works of God, he tries to manipulate what Christians confess and profess out of their mouths.

***

7. *"I never had a personal conviction about it."*

Sometimes, we've looked to our feelings to find conviction. A "personal" conviction is when you decide to [or not to] do something because God has a specific instruction for you. Examples of personal convictions are to keep a certain diet to avoid gluttony or bad eating habits, not wearing a certain type of clothing because it isn't modest for your specific body type, not kissing your boyfriend or girlfriend because it leads you to lust, not watching action movies, and anything else that is not verbatim scripture, but the Holy Spirit has convicted you about it. However, anything that directly violates the Word and commandments of God cannot be acceptable just because of a lack "personal conviction," even if it doesn't make you "feel" bad by doing it. The topic at hand is not a personal conviction because this is based on how God feels about it, according to the Word of God, and not how *we feel* about it.

Conviction is defined as a firmly held belief or opinion.[33] As Christians, everything that the Word says should be our conviction. The Word of God is not up for debate. There is only one truth, revealed by the Holy Spirit of Truth. Much scripture has been given in this book that shows which ways membership in these fraternities and sororities go against God's Word. I strongly advise and encourage fasting about this subject, completely humbling the flesh, and allowing yourself to hear Him clearly. We desire for God to convict us, and He does, especially if we are open to it. I also highly encourage comparing all your Greek material with the Bible side by side and seeing if anything contradicts.

A quote I heard on a denouncing testimony video was, "Just because you don't feel convicted by it, it doesn't mean that it isn't sin."

***

8. *"The organizations are founded on Christian principles."*

Principles are ways of behaviors and attitudes. Many things are founded on Christian principles. This includes charity work, philosophy, American politics, and so much more. Christian principles have always been influential upon society. We see Christian principles to be things that are morally right, and this is good. However, just because something is 'good,' or *includes* godly things does not mean it comes from God. It does not mean that He is pleased. *Mere inclusion does not equal holiness.* My question is: what else are the organizations founded on? Unfortunately, it is not solely Christian principles. The foundation is mixed with all of the pagan and ancient, idolatrous culture discussed thus far. Anything with mixture is not of God because He is holy. In His perfect goodness, He is set apart. Nothing taints Him. He has no fellowship or inclusion with darkness. As the bible tells us to be holy as He is holy, we also must not have fellowship and *inclusion* with darkness. This is why the inclusion of Christian principles is *not enough*. Satan's strategy of deception is to make the Christian feel comfortable that the organizations do good works, pray, attend church, and inform its members that it is founded on Christian principles. It's a *partial truth* presented to the member as the whole truth, as the other founding principles are not jointly being mentioned; that is *deception*.

Speaking of good works, the presence of good works does not mean that being in an organization is good in God's eyes because, again, we are not saved *by* our good works.

9. Lastly, the statement I heard the most, especially when I was in college was, **"It's not that deep."**

It is that deep. We, too often, have thought of this world so physically. Many things truly have a depth and significant impact on our walk with God, especially anything that uses rituals and rites, because the spiritual transcends the natural.

Anything on the heart and mind of God is that deep. Anything in which we are seeing a mass exodus is that deep.

> Some have said,
> "It's just mythology."
> "It's just symbolism, and you'd only understand if you were a member."
> "I don't [personally] worship any other god besides the One true God."
> "It's all about the intent of your heart. I never put my organization above God."
> "There is nothing religious about it."

Even if it is 'just' mythology, God does not even want His people mentioning the names of the gods of the heathens. I'd like to propose that there is a significant difference between speaking the names of other gods, by simply reading about Greek mythology in a secondary school class for example, versus speaking the names of other gods in the context of an actual ritual or initiation. This is because a 'ritual' is spiritual in nature, whether the initiate believes it or not, and usually has an altar involved. Furthermore, these deities are worshiped in real religions and practices outside of fraternities and sororities.

Scriptures

Exodus 23:13 – *"Pay close attention to all My instructions. You must not call on the* **name** *of any other gods.* **Do not even speak their names.***"* (NLT)

Joshua 23:7-8 – *"...lest you go among these nations, these who remain among you. You shall not make mention of the* **name** *of their gods, nor cause anyone to swear by them; you shall not serve them nor bow down to them, but you shall hold fast to the Lord your God, as you have done to this day."*

Context/Explanation of Scripture

Matthew Poole's Commentary:
"**Make no mention**, to wit, with honour or delight, or without detestation… Or, *not mention* them in your worship, or in oaths, or in common discourse, and without special occasion, lest the frequent mention of them might keep up their memory, or introduce their worship. Hence the names of idols and idolatrous places were often changed by the Israelites. See Numbers 32:38, Joshua 23:7; Compare Psalm 16:4, Hosea 2:17, Zechariah 13:2."

Ellicott's Commentary for English Readers:
"**Be circumspect.**—Rather, *take heed*. The verb used is a very common one. **Make no mention of the name of other gods.**—The Jewish commentators understand swearing by the name of other gods to be the thing here forbidden… But the words used reach far beyond this. Contempt for the "gods of the nations" **was to be shown by ignoring their very names.** They were not to be spoken of, unless by preachers in the way of warning, or by historians when the facts of history could not be otherwise set forth. Moses himself mentions Baal (Numbers 22:41), Baal-peor (Numbers 25:3; Numbers 25:5), Chemosh (Numbers 21:29), and Moloch (Leviticus 20:2-5; Leviticus 23:21)."

Exodus 22:20 – *"He who sacrifices to any god, except to the Lord only, he shall be utterly destroyed."*

X. RESOURCES AND STEPS TO DENOUNCE/RENOUNCE

Why is it important to renounce?

Renouncing takes you out of agreement with the covenants you were in. When you joined a GLO, there were different oaths, vows, chants, and hymns you had to speak from your mouth, and different actions you did as well. This was by your free will, which allowed respective covenants to form. Moreover, there was a coming into agreement by way of ceremony, rituals, and oaths. The blood of Jesus, and your free will to obey Him, is enough to break and get these covenants out of your life. By renouncing, you declare and announce in the spiritual realm that you are separated and divorced from these agreements and any associated spirits.

The following resources are quoted from www.outfromamongthem.com, with steps on denouncing and renouncing.

What's the Difference Between Renouncing & Denouncing?

When it comes to leaving a secret society, we are sometimes asked what the difference is between renounce and denounce, so we will briefly explain.

Both words are applicable when coming out of a secret society, which is why you will see them used interchangeably; however, they have different meanings. Renounce means "giving up or abandoning something," while denounce means "to publicly speak against something or someone."

- The word "renounce" is a verb and means "to formally give up a thing." It derives from the French and Latin words "renuncer" and "renuntiare." Additional meanings are formally rejecting, abandoning a viewpoint, or committing to stop doing or having something.
- The word "denounce" is also a verb, and derives from French and Latin words "denuncier" and "denuntiare." Additional meanings are to make known in a formal manner, openly condemn, declare, or proclaim to be cursed, wicked, or evil (e.g., denouncing atheism).

When separating from a secret society, one must acknowledge their sin, repent to GOD, and renounce being part of the organization and all ties to it. To denounce is to share God's truth of how it's incompatible with being a faithful born-again follower of Jesus Christ.

To add to this insight on renouncing and denouncing: some wonder if it is okay to just be an inactive member or a non-financial member instead of going through the entire process of separating from the organization. No, you need to completely separate and withdraw. This will sever any ties and access especially from the physical realm/practical sense. After the renouncement prayer will be steps on physically withdrawing.

1. Repent & Renounce (Prayer example below)

Secret Society Renouncement Prayer

NOTE: This is a guide; as Holy Spirit leads you to repent and renounce other things, please do so earnestly. Out From Among Them Ministries also suggests coupling this prayer with the Freemasonry and Order of Eastern Star (OES) deliverance prayers since all BGLOs derive their rituals from Freemasonry. You can find these prayers under the Resources tab at www.outfromamongthem.com

Father GOD, I come to You humbly, acknowledging Your authority and power and honoring You as Creator of heaven and earth. I confess I have operated in idolatry and chose to follow Satan instead of You and Your Word by joining a secret society or seeking/attempting to join. I repent of all idolatry, taking Your name in vain and the blasphemy attached to being part of a secret society. In the name and power of Jesus Christ alone, I repent and renounce all ungodly covenants and association with Freemasonry, Prince Hall Masonry, Shriners, OES, Illuminati, other lodges and crafts, fraternities, sororities, and any other secret or occult groups pledged and/or joined.

I renounce the spirit of antichrist, spirit of death, and ALL ungodly powers that rule over these organizations. I repent and renounce all forms of paganism and witchcraft I opened myself up to which includes attachments to false gods such as Baal, Baphomet, Osiris, Isis, Horus, Set, Minerva/Athena, Apollo/Apollyon, Anubis, Aurora/Eos, Bastet, Themis, Atlas, _____ (add in any other names of false gods/goddess The Holy Spirit advises of).

I repent and renounce the demonic covenant that took place through oaths and rituals. I repent and renounce every ritual, prayer and hymn I spoke, sung, and agreed to. I repent and renounce the false light mentioned in rituals, which represents Lucifer/ Satan. I repent and renounce the worship of the organization instilled in me through initiation. I renounce the mixing and mingling of truth and error. I acknowledge and repent for accepting mythology, fabrication, and lies taught as truth through these organizations. I repent and renounce every position held in these organizations, for calling or thinking of another as a "master," or any other similar title that is idolatrous to The Most High GOD.

I repent and renounce for taking Your Word in vain. I repent and renounce vain traditions of men by accepting initiations and rituals as truth. I repent and renounce for accepting and reciting twisted versions of GOD's Holy Word made to fit the organization. I repent for swearing an oath to the organization, and laying my hand on The Holy Bible while pledging myself to the organization. I repent and renounce the curse of all hand signs, calls, secret passwords, handshakes, etc., attached to the organization.

I repent and renounce rejection, insecurity, and lack of identity in Jesus Christ. I repent and renounce the love of position and power, the love of acceptance, the love of money, the lust of the flesh, the lust of the eyes, and the pride of life that lead people into these antichrist organizations. I repent and renounce all fear and intimidation released into participants of these organizations through hazing (mental and physical). I repent for harming, intimidating, or retaliating against others.

Through the power of Jesus Christ, I repent and renounce all soul ties from being part of these organizations. I pray all ungodly relationships You did not ordain for my life be removed. I repent and renounce the fear of being alone, fear of man, and the fear of fully trusting in GOD.

I repent and renounce emotional hardness, apathy, indifference, unbelief, bitterness, and anger in Jesus' name. I repent and renounce any anxiety, depression, oppression, obsession, emotional damage, confusion, and extreme fear. I renounce attacks while sleeping, nightmares, and incubus and succubus spirits. I renounce the blinding of spiritual truth, the darkening of the soul, and false imaginations.

I repent and renounce all forms of false beliefs and ancient religions these organizations draw from such as (but not limited to): syncretism, paganism, polytheism, occultism, esotericism, astrology, divination, ancestral worship, voodoo/vodun/hoodoo, Wicca, Satanism, New Age, Jainism, Buddhism, Hinduism, Islam, Kemetism, Black Hebrew Israelism, Mormonism, Jehovah's Witness, Catholicism, Gnosticism, etc.

I confess there is only ONE true GOD, who ALONE is worthy of ALL worship and praise. And ONLY through Jesus Christ, Son of The True and Living GOD, can one obtain remission of sins, freedom, healing, deliverance, and redemption. With that, I start anew today by giving every aspect of myself back to You Jesus; turning completely away from the unrighteousness of these organizations. I humbly thank You Lord all vows, obligations, oaths, penalties, and curses enacted or pronounced against my life and body are severed. I also thank You for continued healing and deliverance as I walk out full submission and obedience to Your Word. I glorify and thank You Father GOD for Your love, mercy, grace, correction and protection. In Jesus' Wonderful Name I pray all these things... AMEN.

2. Remove and Discard

"Remove and discard ALL paraphernalia and references to the organization in your home, car, phone, computer, etc. This includes removing items such as clothing, jewelry, wall art, car tags, pictures, social media posts and videos (you may need to untag yourself as well), etc.

*For physical items, we strongly recommend cutting up or burning them (refer to Acts 19:19 & Deut. 12:3). Please do not give items to anyone as that would be passing along evil and deception to others."

3. Withdraw
(withdrawal template included)

"Send a withdrawal letter to the headquarters of the organization to be officially removed as a member (if applicable, copy the regional leadership as well). This is important to do in full obedience to The Most High God. When joining these organizations it was willingly done in both a spiritual and natural manner; therefore, ensure to sever ties with the organization in the same manner."

If you are told to sign an NDA (non-disclosure agreement), or sign anything for that matter, please note that you are not obliged, to withdraw from the organization. As you are leaving, don't allow them to put you into even more bondage.

SHAMARI PITTS

[Your First and Last Name]
[Full Mailing Address]
[Your Email address]

[Date]
[Name of Organization], Inc.
[Attn: Member Services or contact person]
[Street Address]
[City, State and Zip Code]

RE: Withdrawal of Membership
- Name at time of initiation: [insert name when joined if changed]
- Membership ID: [insert your membership ID]
- Chapter Initiated: [insert chapter name where initiated]
- School Initiated: [insert name of college or university]
- Date Initiated: [insert date]

This letter is to advise that I, [insert name], am requesting that my membership in _____ [insert name of organization] be fully withdrawn and my name be removed from all records as of this _____ day of _____ (month), _____ (Year).

[Insert explanation of why you're withdrawing if you choose to; e.g. I have renounced [insert org name] Inc. because it conflicts with my beliefs as a follower of Christ]

I do not have in my possession any rituals, pins, or paraphernalia to return. OR: Enclosed you will find all items I had in my possession related to this organization. [OR, use whatever applies here]

Please confirm my removal or provide the necessary next steps to facilitate my official removal.

_____   _____
Signature   Date

NOTARY [insert only if needed]

State of _____
County of _____, to-wit:
I, _____, a Notary Public of the above-referenced jurisdiction do hereby certify that _____, hereby appeared before me and signed this affidavit on the _____ day of _____ (month), _____ (Year). I examined the following type of identification: _____.

_____
Notary Public Signature

My Commission Expires:

_____
INSERT SEAL/STAMP

4. Share Testimony

"Share your testimony and God's Truth with others. Our testimonies glorify The Most High God first and foremost (Revelation 12:11).It also aids in leading others to the truth about these organizations, and prayerfully confirms for someone to repent and renounce as well."

XI. TESTIMONIES

Please scan the QR code above to view real-life testimonies from two amazing individuals who left their previous organizations in obedience to the Lord. God continues doing amazing things in their lives! Below is information about them, including short excerpts from the full videos.

ASHTON ASRES

Minister • Communicator
YouTube: @TheSecretPlaceNetwork | Instagram: @ashtonasres

"When we were bowing at that altar during our initiation process, we were bowing to the god, Apollo. Many are unaware of this shrine because when you're going through the initiation process, you don't have the ritual book... a lot of times, you're just repeating what you're being told to say... you're unaware of what you're doing; you're unaware of the covenant and the oaths that you are making and taking.... When the Lord began to reveal these things to me, my heart became very grieved. I had to go through a process of renouncing in the spirit...

The journey has been worth it..."

***

AKIRA CA'PRI

Minister
YouTube: @AkiraCapri | Instagram: @akira.capri | TikTok: @akira.capri

"The part everyone has to go through... the initiation part.. going in a dark room, signing your [name] at an altar, kneeling before... saying bible verses in the name of AKA, literally scriptures taken out of the bible but put in Alpha Kappa Alpha; that broke Him; I was weeping... This is enough for me, to know how I broke His heart...

God is pressing it on your heart to pick Him; the One and Only True and Living God, He wants you to come out of deception. He loves you just that much..."

References

A.E.A.O.N.M.S. History of A.E.A.O.N.M.S. The Ancient Egyptian Arabic Order Nobles Mystic Shrine of North and South America and Its Jurisdictions, Inc. https://aeaonms.org/history/

Anointed Vessel. (2009). So Why You Ain't Pledgin Part Deux. Anointedvessel's Weblog. https://anointedvessel.wordpress.com/2009/05/07/so-why-you-aint-pledgin-part-deux/11/

Art of the Root. (2023, September 25). The Art of Casting the Magic Circle. https://artoftheroot.com/blogs/news/casting-a-circle

Beta Alpha Chapter, Phi Beta Sigma Fraternity Incorporated. (n.d.). The History of Stepping according to the Temple of Blue. https://www.ba1935.com/history-of-stepping

Britannica, T. Editors of Encyclopedia (2011, September 16). altar. Encyclopedia Britannica. https://www.britannica.com/topic/altar

Britannica, T. Editors of Encyclopedia (2024, July 16). Delphic oracle. Encyclopedia Britannica. https://www.britannica.com/topic/Delphic-oracle

Burlington Camden Alumni Chapter Kappa Alpha Psi Fraternity, Inc. (n.d.). The Chapter Invisible, In Remembrance of those Who Have Preceded us to the Golden Shore. https://kappasofburlcam.com/the-chapter-invisible/

Cable, Eric. (2012). Masonic Square and Compasses. English Wikipedia, Wikimedia Commons. https://commons.wikimedia.org/wiki/File:Masonic_SquareCompassesG.svg

Canadian Museum of History. (n.d.). Engine Search: Egyptian civilization – Architecture – Sphinx. Accessed April 15, 2023.

https://www.historymuseum.ca > cmc > civil > egypt

Capoccia, T. (n.d.). The Question of Freemasonry. Bible Bulletin Board. https://www.biblebb.com/files/masons.htm

Carruth, William H. (1909). Each in his own Tongue (New York: G. P. Putnam's Sons, The Knickerbocker Press, 1909): 2-3. 9700.d.146 Cambridge University Library.

Crump, William L. (1983). THE STORY OF KAPPA ALPHA PSI, A History of the Beginning and Development of a College Greek Letter Organization 1911-1983 Third Edition. Accessed October 10, 2024 from https://brittlebooks.library.illinois.edu/brittlebooks_closed/Books2009-04/crumwi0001stokap/crumwi0001stokap.pdf

De Lorenzo, KufoletoAntonio and Ventayol, Marina. (2007). Delphi tholos cazzul. CC BY 3.0 <https://creativecommons.org/licenses/by/3.0>, via Wikimedia Commons. https://commons.wikimedia.org/wiki/File:Delphi_tholos_cazzul.JPG

Delta Sigma Theta, Inc., Grand Chapter. (1987-1990). Membership Intake Program. Information accessed via https://www.dontgogreek.com/downloads/DSTSTD.pdf

Delta Sigma Theta, Inc. (1987-1990). DST Grand Chapter Candidate Syllabus. Information accessed via https://www.dontgogreek.com/downloads/BiblicallyUnravelling.pdf

Delta Sigma Theta, Inc. (1996). The Official Ritual of the Grand Chapter of Delta Sigma Theta Sorority, Inc. Information accessed via https://www.dontgogreek.com/downloads/DSTSTD.pdf

Durham (NC) Alumni Chapter of Kappa Alpha Psi. (n.d.) The Kappa

Alpha Psi Hymn. https://kapsida.tripod.com/nationals/hymn.htm

Ehrmann, M. & Ehrmann, B. P. Desiderata.

Ephesians 5:11, Inc. 1996-2016. How can you lead Masons away from the Masonic Lodge? http://www.ephesians5-11.org/

Epsilon Epsilon Chapter, Iota Phi Theta Fraternity Incorporated (n.d.). Birth of Iota. Retrieved September 20, 2024, from https://epsilonepsiloniotas.weebly.com/symbols--insignia.html#:~:text=A%20Mythical%20beast%20with%20the,are%20referred%20to%20as%20Centaurs

1st Step Media. (2018, April 30). I see the light. YouTube. h https://www.youtube.com/watch?v=g4DAZpZhARo

Gamma Upsilon Chapter. (2015). Lyrics. *Dear Kappa Alpha Psi.* https://mightygammaupsilon.com/1707-2/. https://mightygammaupsilon.com/wp-content/uploads/2015/10/dear-kappaalpha-psi-sheetmusic.jpg

Gamma Upsilon Chapter. (2015). Lyrics. *For Kappa Alpha Psi.* https://mightygammaupsilon.com/1707-2/. https://mightygammaupsilon.com/wp-content/uploads/2015/10/kappa-poem.jpg

Gamma Upsilon Chapter. (2015). Lyrics. *Kappa Alpha Psi March.* https://mightygammaupsilon.com/1707-2/. https://mightygammaupsilon.com/wp-content/uploads/2015/10/kappa-march.jpg

Gamma Upsilon Chapter. (2015). Lyrics. *The Diamond.* https://mightygammaupsilon.com/1707-2/. https://mightygammaupsilon.com/wp-content/uploads/2015/10/the-damond.jpg

Gamma Upsilon Chapter. (2015). Lyrics. *The Scrollers Hymn.*

https://mightygammaupsilon.com/1707-2/.
https://mightygammaupsilon.com/wp-content/uploads/2015/10/scrollers-hymn.jpg

Gentil, J. (2016). A Survey of Undergraduate Fraternities Founded by Masons. The Greek Rite. The Scottish Rite Journal. 8-11. https://pubs.royle.com/publication/?m=22869&i=328085&p=10&ver=html5

Grand Lodge of Ancient, Free & Accepted Masons of Oregon Washington Masonic Lodge No. 46 A. F. & A. M. (2017, January). Masonic Light. https://washington46.org/2017/01/30/masonic-light/

Guzik, David. (n.d.). Colossians 2 – Answering the Colossian Heresy. The Enduring Word Commentary. Accessed October 19, 2024. https://enduringword.com/bible-commentary/colossians-2/#top

Hatchett. (2005, December 4). Exposing Delta Sigma Theta. GLO's Exposed Discussion Forum. https://pub6.bravenet.com/forum/static/show.php?usernum=460887521&frmid=66&msgid=616355

Henley, William E. (1875). Invictus. Poems (London: Macmillan and Co., 1920): 83-84. Public domain.

Horner, W. (2004, November 13). "Alpha Hymn." https://alphaforlife.org/Alpha_Hymn.html

Horntip, J. (2001) Sister's Keeper. Black Greek Soundz (2001). The Jack Horntip Collection. https://www.horntip.com/mp3/2000s/2001ca_black_greek_soundz_songs_and_chants_(CDs)/2001ca_sigma_gamma_rho_sorority/12_i_am_my_sisters_keeper.htm

Kappa Alpha Nu Journal. (Vol 1, No 1. 1914). https://online.flippingbook.com/view/115633/2/

Lahners, D.A. (2021, October). In Defense of the Hot Sands (Among other things). The Midnight Freemasons. http://www.midnightfreemasons.org/2021/10/in-defense-of-hot-sands-amongother.html

Leonid 2. (2023). Centaur with snake tail. CC BY-SA 3.0 <https://creativecommons.org/licenses/by-sa/3.0>, via Wikimedia Commons. https://commons.wikimedia.org/wiki/File:Centaur_with_snake_tail.svg

Ma, Connie. (2014). Louvre Museum, CC BY-SA 2.0 <https://creativecommons.org/licenses/by-sa/2.0>, via Wikimedia Commons. https://commons.wikimedia.org/wiki/File:Sphinx,_Louvre_15_June_2014.jpg

Merchang, D., & Rich, P. (2001, April 7). Freemasonry, the Greeks, and Stepping. The National Conference on Stepping. https://studylib.net/doc/8345628/freemasonry--the-greeks--and-stepping

Merkur, D. (2024, September 19). mysticism. Encyclopedia Britannica. https://www.britannica.com/topic/mysticism

Moneyhon, C. (2023, October 31). Albert Pike (1809–1891). Central Arkansas Library System (CALS) Encyclopedia of Arkansas. Accessed October 17, 2024. https://encyclopediaofarkansas.net/entries/albert-pike-1737/#:~:text=After%20he%20ceased%20practicing%20law,Priest%20from%201853%20to%201854.

MrGomab60. (2011, August 6). Sgma Crescent Chant: Oh Sigma Dear. YouTube. https://www.youtube.com/watch?v=pcbiBxgB09A

National Museum of African American History & Culture (NMAAHC). Prince Hall Masons. https://www.searchablemuseum.com/prince-hall-masons

Newman, P.D. (2014, June 12). The Symbol of the Skull and Crossbones and Its Masonic Application. Knight Templar Magazine Index. https://www.knightstemplar.org/KnightTemplar/articles/20130523.htm#Top

Out From Among Them Ministries (OFATM). Darkness Exposed. Accessed Spring 2024; page inactive on 27 September 2024. https://www.outfromamongthem.com/darknessexposed

Out From Among Them Ministries (OFATM). FAQs & Common Rebuttals. https://www.outfromamongthem.com/faqs

Out From Among Them Ministries (OFATM). Ministry Resources. https://www.outfromamongthem.com/resources

Pavielle. (2024). Overcoming Deception: Why I Had To Denounce Delta Sigma Theta Sorority. https://pavielle.com/delta-sigma-theta/

Pike, A. (1871). Morals and Dogma of the Ancient and Accepted Scottish Rite of Freemasonry. Google Books. Accessed October 18, 2024. https://books.google.com/books?id=VQ4RAdCRHb0C&pg=PA2&source=kp_read_button&hl=en&newbks=1&newbks_redir=0#v=onepage&q&f=false

Renee. (n.d.) http://ms_quiet.tripod.com/chants.html

Rice, J. (2006). Can You Be a Christian and Greek?: An in-depth analysis of Black Greek Letter Organizations. https://www.dontgogreek.com/downloads/GLOexpose.pdf

Richards, D. (2015) . The origins of the tomb. Yale Alumni Magazine. https://yalealumnimagazine.org/articles/4072-the-origins-of-the-tomb

Scottish Rite Freemasonry, Northern Masonic Jurisdiction (NMJ).

(n.d.). A Brief History of Prince Hall Freemasonry. Scottish Rite Blog. https://scottishritenmj.org/blog/prince-hall-freemasonry

Secrecy. (Winter 1994). Royal Arch Mason. 18(4), 118.

Simpson, A. (n.d.). The Alpha Phi Alpha Hymn. https://alphaforlife.org/Alpha_Hymn.html

Skip Tarrant. (2019, June 1). "How does someone become a Wiccan high priest or priestess, and what do they do?" Quora. https://www.quora.com/How-does-someone-become-a-Wiccan-high-priest-or-priestess-and-what-do-they-do/answer/Skip-Tarrant

Smithsonian Digital Volunteers: Transcription Center. (Last Update: 2017, September 4). Sorority and Fraternity Songs. Accessed October 13, 2024. https://transcription.si.edu/view/10853/NMAAHC-2012_31_5_011

Stafford, D. (2007, June 9). Freemasonry and the Development of Greek-Letter Fraternities. Tennessee Lodge of Research. Retrieved from http://tnlor.org/?p=24

Stephey, M.J. (2009, February 23). The Skull & Bones Society. Time Magazine. https://web.archive.org/web/20090226150130/http://www.time.com/time/nati on/article/0,8599,1881172,00.html OR….. https://time.com/archive/6914131/the-skull-bones-society/

The Boule. (n.d.). Nurturers of Knowledge, nurturersofknowledge.weebly.com. https://nurturersofknowledge.weebly.com/uploads/2/2/7/3/22738286/56630464-the-boule.pdf

The Hymn of Iota Phi Theta. (n.d.) Lyrics by Richard Johnson. file:///C:/Users/18455/Downloads/iotahymn%20(2).pdf

The Mu Beta Chapter of Sigma Gamma Rho Sorority, Inc. (n.d.) Sigma Gamma Rho Sorority, Inc Chants. https://www.angelfire.com/tn2/mubeta/index7.html

Upsilon Omega Chapter Omega Psi Phi Fraternity, Inc. Graduate Chapter St. Louis, MO. (n.d.) Hymn of the Omega Psi Phi Fraternity, Inc. https://www.angelfire.com/mo/upsilonomegapsiphi/hymn.html

Watch the Yard. (2024, January 23). Iota Phi Theta Founder Lonnie C. Spurill Jr. Just Became a Master Mason. https://www.watchtheyard.com/iotas/iota-phi-theta-lonnie-c-spurill-jr-just-became-a-master-mason/

Wesley, C.H. (1969). History of Sigma Pi Phi: First of the Negro-American Greek-Letter Fraternities.

"Why Pledge a Fraternity?" at http://www.geocities.com/Athens/Agora/9223/Greeks.html

Wigington, P. (2018, March 14). How to Cast a Circle for a Pagan Ritual. Learn Religions. https://www.learnreligions.com/how-to-cast-a-circle-2562859

Wikipedia Commons. (2010). Ο Ἄρης (Borghese-Λούβρου). Wikipedia Commons, CC BY-SA 4.0 <https://creativecommons.org/licenses/by-sa/4.0>, via Wikimedia Commons. https://commons.wikimedia.org/wiki/File:%CE%9F_%CE%86%CF%81%CE%B7%CF%82_(Borghese-%CE%9B%CE%BF%CF%8D%CE%B2%CF%81%CE%BF%CF%85).jpg

Winston, Allen. (2003). The Great Sphinx of Giza: An Introduction. Retrieved January 23, 2007. https://www.newworldencyclopedia.org/entry/Sphinx

Footnotes

1. divine. (n.d.). In Merriam-Webster.com. Retrieved September 15, 2024, from https://www.merriam-webster.com/dictionary/divine
2. hellenism. (n.d.). In Merriam-Webster.com. Retrieved September 15, 2024, from https://www.merriam-webster.com/dictionary/Hellenism
3. hellenism. (July 2023). In OED.com. Retrieved September 15, 2024, from https://doi.org/10.1093/OED/8333140073
4. ritual. (June 2024). In OED.com. Retrieved September 15, 2024, from Google search: "ritual definition;" https://doi.org/10.1093/OED/9041082572
5. altar. (September 2024). In OED.com. Retrieved September 15, 2024, from https://doi.org/10.1093/OED/9052484642
6. hymn. (n.d.). In OED.com. Retrieved September 15, 2024, from Google search: "hymn definition;" https://doi.org/10.1093/OED/6552448268
7. [a] hymn. (n.d.). In Biblehub.com. Retrieved September 15, 2024, from https://biblehub.com/greek/5215.htm
8. worship. (n.d.). In Merriam-Webster.com. Retrieved September 15, 2024, from https://www.merriam-webster.com/dictionary/worship
9. worship. (September 2024). In OED.com. Retrieved September 15, 2024, from https://doi.org/10.1093/OED/1002193039
10. idolatry. (July 2023). In OED.com. Retrieved September 15, 2024, from Google search: "idolatry definition;" https://doi.org/10.1093/OED/7100890247
11. Britannica, T. Editors of Encyclopedia (2024, May 23). secret society. Encyclopedia Britannica. https://www.britannica.com/topic/secret-society
12. Britannica, T. Editors of Encyclopedia (2024, September 10). Freemasonry. Encyclopedia Britannica. https://www.britannica.com/topic/Freemasonry
13. kneel. (September 2024). In OED.com. Retrieved October 9, 2024, from Google search: "kneel definition;"

https://doi.org/10.1093/OED/1236705482

14. Alpha Phi Alpha Fraternity, Incorporated. (1976, Reprint). Ritual of the Alpha Phi Alpha Fraternity Incorporated. Issued by the General Office, Chicago, Illinois. Accessed October 9, 2024, from https://www.scribd.com/document/408002025/ritual-of-alpha-phi-alpha-pdf and https://www.stichtingargus.nl/vrijmetselarij/g/alphaphialpha_r.html

15. Alpha Kappa Alpha Sorority. (August 1977). Rituals (Revised, August 1977). Accessed October 9, 2024, from https://www.scribd.com/document/407197006/ritual-of-alpha-kappa-alpha-pdf and https://www.stichtingargus.nl/vrijmetselarij/g/alphakappaalpha_r.html

16. Delta Sigma Theta Sorority, Incorporated. (before 2021). Official Ritual 12th Edition. Retrieved April 8, 2024, via hard copy.

17. Zeta Phi Beta Initiation Ritual. (1994). Accessed October 9, 2024, via PDF from https://www.stichtingargus.nl/vrijmetselarij/g/zetaphibeta_r.html

18. Sigma Gamma Rho Rituals. (n.d.). Accessed October 9, 2024, from https://www.stichtingargus.nl/vrijmetselarij/g/sigmagammarho_r.html

19. Omega Psi Phi Initiation Ritual. (n.d.). Accessed October 9, 2024, from https://www.scribd.com/document/362736614/omega-psi-phi-docx

20. Phi Beta Sigma Initiation Ritual. (n.d.). Accessed October 9, 2024, via PDF from https://www.stichtingargus.nl/vrijmetselarij/g/phibetasigma_r.html

21. Kappa Alpha Psi Initiation Ritual. (1968). Accessed October 9, 2024, via PDF from https://www.stichtingargus.nl/vrijmetselarij/g/kappaalphapsi_r2.html

22. The Constitution and Statutes of Kappa Alpha Psi Fraternity, Inc. (2007). *78th Grand Chapter Meeting*. Accessed October 9, 2024, via

PDF from file:///C:/Users/18455/Downloads/Updated_Constitution_and_Statutes_of_Kappa_Alpha_Psi_Fraternity%20(4).pdf and file:///C:/Users/18455/Downloads/Kappa_Constitution_(UPDATED)%20(4).pdf

23. oracle. (n.d.) In Merriam-Webster.com. Retrieved October 9, 2024, from https://www.merriam-webster.com/dictionary/oracle
24. G1497 - eidōlon - Strong's Greek Lexicon (nkjv). Retrieved from https://www.blueletterbible.org/lexicon/g1497/nkjv/tr/0-1/
25. Delta Sigma Theta Initiation Ritual. (1969). Accessed October 10, 2024, via PDF from https://www.stichtingargus.nl/vrijmetselarij/g/deltasigmatheta_r.html
26. subjugate. (September 2023). In OED.com. Retrieved September 25, 2024, from https://doi.org/10.1093/OED/7337359892
27. mantra. (n.d.). In Merriam-Webster.com. Retrieved September 26, 2024, from https://www.merriam-webster.com/dictionary/mantra
28. mantra. (June 2024). In OED.com. Retrieved September 26, 2024, from Google search: "mantra definition;" https://doi.org/10.1093/OED/9685642940
29. Porte, C. (2024, July). Exposing the "Centaur Ceremony" of Iota Phi Theta Fraternity, Inc. YouTube. Accessed September 19, 2024. (link unavailable).
30. esotericism. (n.d.). In Merriam-Webster.com. Retrieved September 27, 2024, from https://www.merriam-webster.com/dictionary/esotericism
31. mystical. (March 2024). In OED.com. Retrieved September 27, 2024, from Google search: "mystical definition;" https://doi.org/10.1093/OED/1007919313
32. tenet. (n.d.). In Merriam-Webster.com dictionary. Retrieved September 27, 2024, from https://www.merriam-webster.com/dictionary/tenet
33. oath. (September 2024). In OED.com. Retrieved October 10, 2024, from Google search: "oath definition" and https://doi.org/10.1093/OED/7256271698

34. conviction. (March 2024). In OED.com. Retrieved October 10, 2024, from Google search: "conviction definition;" https://doi.org/10.1093/OED/6261328509

ABOUT THE AUTHOR

Shamari Pitts is a Belizean-American writer currently residing in the Dallas-Fort Worth Metroplex. Her debut book, "It's That Deep," was birthed out of a passion for biblical teaching, research, writing, and seeing God's people flourish. When she isn't writing, you can find her singing and worshipping, studying psychology, exploring culture, and being a "professional" foodie. Keep in touch with Shamari and her adventures! Her creative projects, vlog content, and email can be found at shamaripitts.com

www.ingramcontent.com/pod-product-compliance
Lightning Source LLC
Chambersburg PA
CBHW050519100526
44581CB00001B/17